W9-CXL-761

LAS VEGAS WITH KIDS

BE A TRAVELER - NOT A TOURIST!

CRITICAL ACCLAIM FOR
OPEN ROAD TRAVEL GUIDES!

Whether you're going abroad or planning a trip in the United States, take Open Road along on your journey. Our books have been praised by **Travel & Leisure, The Los Angeles Times, Newsday, Booklist, US News & World Report, Endless Vacation, American Bookseller, Coast to Coast,** *and many other magazines and newspapers!*

Don't just see the world – experience it with Open Road!

ABOUT THE AUTHORS

Paris Permenter and John Bigley, a husband-wife travel writing team, are the authors of Open Road Publishing's *Las Vegas with Kids, Caribbean with Kids*, and *National Parks with Kids*. The team have also authored numerous other books, including travel guides to the Leeward Islands, the Cayman Islands, Jamaica and other Caribbean destinations. They have contributed many articles to leading travel magazines and newspapers, and are frequent television and radio talk show guests on the subject of travel. Readers can follow the couple's travels on their websites: Travels with Paris and John *(www.parisandjohn.com)* and Lovetripper Romantic Travel Magazine *(www.lovetripper.com)*.

HIT THE OPEN ROAD – WITH OPEN ROAD PUBLISHING!

Open Road Publishing now has guide books to exciting, fun destinations on four continents. As veteran travelers, our goal is to bring you the best travel guides available anywhere!

No small task, but here's what we offer:

• All Open Road travel guides are written by authors with a distinct, opinionated point of view – not some sterile committee or team of writers. Our authors are experts in the areas covered and are polished writers.

• Our guides are geared to people who want great vacations, great value, and great tips for both standard tourist sights *and* fun, unique alternatives.

• We're strong on the basics, but we also provide terrific choices for those looking to get off the beaten path and *experience* the country or city – not just *see* it or pass through it.

• We give you the best, but we also tell you about the worst and what to avoid. Nobody should waste their time and money on their hard-earned vacation because of bad or inadequate travel advice.

• Our guides assume nothing. We tell you everything you need to know to have the trip of a lifetime – presented in a fun, literate, nononsense style.

• And, above all, we welcome your input, ideas, and suggestions to help us put out the best travel guides possible.

LAS VEGAS WITH KIDS

BE A TRAVELER - NOT A TOURIST!

Paris Permenter & John Bigley

OPEN ROAD PUBLISHING

OPEN ROAD PUBLISHING

We offer travel guides to American and foreign locales. Our books tell it like it is, often with an opinionated edge, and our experienced authors always give you all the information you need to have the trip of a lifetime. Write for your free catalog of all our titles, including our golf and restaurant guides.

Catalog Department, Open Road Publishing
P.O. Box 284, Cold Spring Harbor, NY 11724

E-mail:
Jopenroad@aol.com

1st Edition

Library of Congress Control No. 00-134107
ISBN 1-892975-37-8

TABLE OF CONTENTS

8. WHAT CAN I BUY?   148

9. WHO'S GOING TO TAKE CARE OF ME?   150

10. DO I HAVE TO GO TO BED?   153

11. DO WE HAVE TO GO HOME ALREADY?   160

SIDEBARS

LAS VEGAS WITH KIDS

INTRODUCTION

Looking for a sure bet for your next vacation? Parents who have previously vacationed in Las Vegas are discovering the fun of introducing their children to this glittery city. Families are playing together and staying together in some of the city's premier hotels, creating vacation memories that will last for generations.

Throughout Las Vegas, you'll find theme hotels that will interest children of all ages. Some provide kids' programs to keep youngsters busy and happy; others offer fun for the whole family in the form of arcades, theme parks, high-tech theaters, and family-friendly shows.

At one time, Las Vegas was definitely an adults-only playland — a place to toss aside your cares as easily as tossing a pair of dice. Luxurious casino hotels welcomed vacationers into a travel fantasyland.

But those travelers are now returning to Las Vegas with the kids in hand. They're finding resorts which welcome the family, places where you'll find rooms with cribs, restaurants with kids' menus, and places to play where the odds of winning are definitely in your favor.

Throughout this book, we've selected the places where your children—whether toddlers or teens—will feel welcome. We'll cruise the Strip and have a look at a city where volcanos erupt just down the street from the New York skyline and the Eiffel Tower. We'll take you back to ancient Egypt, the Roman empire, and the days of King Arthur then whisk you into the future aboard a starship. Let's explore the rainforests, take a Venetian gondola ride, and visit King Tut's tomb, all without a passport. When it's time to head out of town, we'll show you day trips galore in and around the city where you and your family can explore the desert, head to the mountains, or visit historic ghost towns.

Whatever you want from your family vacation, Las Vegas can deliver— in style and within a budget. With its full menu of vacation options, families definitely hold the winning hand in this city.

1. PLANNING YOUR TRIP

WHY LAS VEGAS?

To the world's travelers, Las Vegas is a land of glitter and gold. Its famous Strip shines night and day with endless slot machines, miles of flashing neon, and equally flashy showgirls. Casinos tempt vacationers with gaming tables, top name entertainers and world-class food.

In the late 1980s, Las Vegas decided that it would attract not just adults but families as well. Following the lead of Circus Circus, the city soon touted itself as a place not just as an adult Disneyland but as a place where the whole family could enjoy a vacation. Roller coasters soon accompanied roulette wheels.

And the idea failed.

The world wanted, with good reason, a place where adults could be adults. Where you could stay up all night, eat and drink far more than you should, and try your hand with Lady Luck. The glittery city returned to what it does best – offering a fantasyland for adult travelers.

But much of that fantasyland is also attractive to children. And travelers to Las Vegas – whether they've come as conventioneers

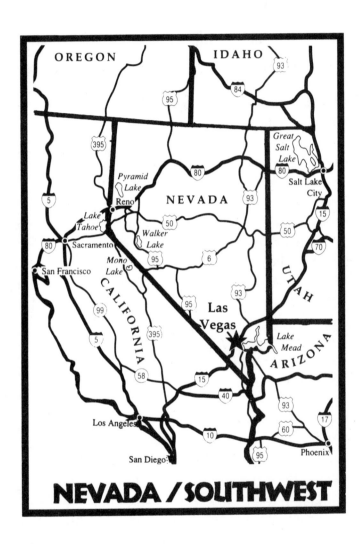

NEVADA / SOUTHWEST

with the family, as a stopover on the way to a California vacation, or as a destination in itself – do bring their families.

So what's the solution? The city has reached a happy medium. Today families represent a second market for Las Vegas. The number one market remains adults, but whether you're coming with toddlers or teens, you will find activities and attractions of interest to the family.

But the key is, like this book title, Las Vegas *with* Kids, it's not Las Vegas *for* Kids. Unlike resorts elsewhere, there are few supervised children's centers in Las Vegas. There are some (more on those in Chapter 9), as well as licensed baby-sitters you can often book through the hotel. But for the most part, you'll want to experience Las Vegas *with* your children. Teens may want to go out on their own some, and there are many arcades that will entertain young travelers while you sneak away to the tables and the slot machines for a few hours, but in general you'll want to experience all this town has to offer together.

And that, after all, is what a family vacation is all about.

CITY HISTORY

Yes, there was a Las Vegas before there was a single slot machine here. OK, it wasn't *much* of a city and once gaming came to town there was no looking back. Today the city is one of the fastest growing areas in the country and tourism is hitting all-time record highs.

Vegas Timeline
1829 Spanish explorers make the first European discovery of the region
1855 Mormon settlers found first settlement in Las Vegas

TOP 10 REASONS TO VISIT LAS VEGAS WITH KIDS

1. **Good prices:** *OK, you won't find single-digit room prices, but you will find good bargains in this city at some of the country's nicest hotels.*

2. **A true fantasyland:** *Las Vegas is unlike any other destination in the world. This is a real fantasyland – where else can you be beamed into outer space, travel back to ancient Egypt, and join in Rio's Carnavale just minutes apart?*

3. **Good weather:** *The best bet in town is the weather. Sure, winter days may be a little chilly for swimming but you won't be shoveling snow off the rental car. And summer days may be downright toasty (make that burnt toast) but you will appreciate those lavish hotel pools (plus every building you'll enter is ultra-air-conditioned, sometimes a little too much!)*

4. **Good family-oriented shows:** *Yes, there are still plenty of silicon shows in town, but Las Vegas has good family-oriented shows as well. Some of the world's best magicians perform here and are usually great options for kids.*

5. **Numerous free attractions:** *Put away the pocketbook, Vegas has plenty of free entertainment as well. More on that later!*

6. **Excellent nearby day trips:** *When it's time to get out of town, active families find white-water rafting, ghost towns, and plenty of desert fun. Check out the "Do We Have to Go Home Already?" chapter for more on those getaways.*

7. **Vegas buffets:** *This town gives new meaning to all-you-can-eat buffets. The spreads in Las Vegas put those anywhere else to shame, usually at prices you can't beat. Even the pickiest eater in the family will be happy.*

8. **Mega-hotels:** *The new crop of casino hotels are an attraction in themselves. Even if you aren't a guest at the property, make time to see some of these one-of-a-kind hotels. We've given you a full rundown of the top family casino hotels in "Which One is My Room?"*

9. **Rides, rides, rides:** *State-of-the-art rides here range from roller coasters to motion theater rides.*

10. **Themes, themes, themes:** *No place can carry a theme like Las Vegas. From King Arthur's court to Venice to Paris, this city takes a theme and runs with it.*

1905 Town of Las Vegas established

1911 City of Las Vegas incorporated

1926 First commercial airline flight (Western Airlines)

1931 Construction of Hoover Dam started

1931 Gambling legalized in the state of Nevada

1941 El Rancho Las Vegas opens on Las Vegas Strip

1946 Bugsy Siegal opens Flamingo Hotel

1966 Howard Hughes moves to Desert Inn

1985 First National Finals Rodeo moves to Las Vegas

1990 Excalibur opens as world's largest hotel

1993 MGM Grand Hotel and Theme Park opens as largest resort
   hotel-casino in world

1994 Work begins on Fremont Street Experience

1995 Fremont Street Experience opens

1998 Bellagio opens as the most expensive hotel in the world ($1.7
   billion)

FACTS & FIGURES

Population of Las Vegas: 436,077

Population of Clark County: 1.2 million

Growth: the county is growing at a rate of 5-8,000 new residents per month

Churches: over 500 churches

Cabs: There are over 1000 taxis in Las Vegas.

Air Travel: Las Vegas McCarran International Airport is North America's 13th busiest.

Name: Las Vegas means "The Meadows" and Nevada means "snowcapped" in Spanish.

Size: The city of Las Vegas covers just over 84 square miles.

WEATHER

Since you're bringing the family, you're probably going to be visiting Las Vegas during the summer months. We're going to give you the weather prediction in one word: **HOT!**

With that in mind, you can prepare. Remember how they always say "it's not the heat, it's the humidity"? Well, at least in Las Vegas you won't have to deal with humidity. With a humidity level of about 29%, this is considered an arid climate.

VEGAS WEATHER

Here's a rundown of typical high/low temperatures you can expect in the city:

	High	Low
January	56	32
February	62	37
March	68	42
April	78	50
May	88	59
June	98	68
July	104	75
August	102	73
September	94	65
October	81	53
November	66	40
December	57	33

And you probably won't have to worry about rain: the city receives just a hair over four inches of rainfall every year. Topped off with 294 days of sunshine a year, the weather gives you just about the best odds in town.

You can see from the weather chart on the previous page that you'll need to carry a coat if your family visits during the winter months and even a light jacket during warm weather months when the temperature falls during the evening hours. (Another benefit of low humidity levels.)

Outside the city, you'll find lower temperatures. If you are considering a day trip up to Mount Charleston (one we'll cover in the final chapter later in this book and highly recommend), you will find the temperatures quite a bit lower than in Vegas (see temperature chart for this excursion in Chapter 11).

DRESSING

Las Vegas is, thankfully, casual. You'll be able to go just about anywhere you like in shorts, t-shirts and jeans. For some special evenings out, however, you will want to carry a nice outfit for everyone in the family. Jackets and ties are not necessary at any of the family-friendly establishments, but for some shows and a few of the restaurants you'll feel more comfortable in a sundress or pair of khaki slacks.

Here are some recommended packing lists:

Family Necessities
• airline tickets
• sunscreen (usually two bottles of different strengths)
• aloe vera lotion for sunburn
• First Aid Kit
• film and camera, extra camera battery
• Cooler (particularly if you're driving to Las Vegas)
• Driver's license and insurance card for car rental
• all prescriptions (in prescription bottles)
• Swimsuit (we usually take two each)

- Mini-address book
- 2 pairs of sunglasses each
- paperback book or two
- first aid kit with aspirin, stomach medicine, bandages, children's aspirin, etc.
- diaper and baby necessities if applicable
- postage stamps

For a four night stay

His packing list:
- 1 pair casual slacks
- 1 pair nice slacks or khakis
- 2 T-shirts
- 2 polo or short sleeve shirts
- 2 pair of shorts
- 2 swimsuits
- 1 pair walking shoes, socks
- 1 pair sandals or tennis shoes

Her packing list:
- 1 pair casual slacks
- 1 casual skirt or 1 dress
- 1 T-shirt
- 2 short sleeve or sleeveless blouses
- 2 pair of shorts
- 2 swimsuits
- 1 pair walking sandals
- 1 pair evening sandals
- 1 swimsuit cover-up

Kids packing list
- 3 pair shorts
- 1 pair jeans or casual pants if you'll be horseback riding
- 3 T-shirts

- 1 old t-shirt to wear while swimming
- 2 dinner outfits, similar to school clothes
- 2 swimsuits (one to wear and one to dry)
- 1 pair sandals
- 1 pair sneakers
- 1 pair swim shoes

INFORMATION SOURCES

There's a wealth of information on Las Vegas available from the Las Vegas Convention and Visitors Authority. For rates and reservation information on hotels and motels in Las Vegas, you can check with the **Las Vegas Convention and Visitors Authority Reservations Department**, *Tel. 702/386-0770 or 800/332-5333.* The reservation center hours are Monday-Saturday 7am-7pm, Sunday 8:30am-6pm.

While in Las Vegas, you can stop by the visitors center. The office can provide you with free brochures and maps, information on RV parks and campsites, museums, dining, shopping, special events, shows, and transportation. The visitors center is found at:

Las Vegas Visitor Information Center
3150 Paradise Rd.
Las Vegas, NV 89109-9096
Tel. 702/892-7575

Outside Las Vegas, you'll find visitor information centers in these Nevada cities:

Boulder City Visitor Information Center
100 Nevada Hwy.
Boulder City, NV 89005
Tel. 702/294-1252

Jean Visitor Information Center
I-15 S., Exit 12, State Rte. 101 E.
Jean, NV 89019
Tel. 702/874-1360

Laughlin Visitor Information Center
1555 Casino Dr.
Laughlin, NV 89029
Tel. 702/298-3321

Mesquite Visitor Information Center
460 North Sandhill Boulevard
Mesquite, NV 89027
Tel. 702/346-2702

Outside Nevada, visitor information centers can also be found in these US cities:

Midwest Region
Two Prudential Plaza
180 N. Stetson
Chicago, IL 60601
Tel. 312/861-0711

Eastern Region
1050 Connecticut Ave., NW
Suite 201
Washington, DC 20036
Tel. 202/296-5300

Outside the US, these cities provide help for international visitors:

Okada Associates
Gyoen Building 8F

1-5-6 Shinjuku
Shinjuku-ku, Tokyo 160-0022, Japan
Tel. 03-3358-3265
Fax 03-3358-3287

Cellet Travel Services
Brook House
47 High St.
Henley in Arden
Warwickshire B95 5AA United Kingdom
Tel. 01564-79-4999
Fax 01564-79-5333

Mangum Management GmbH
Herzogspitalstr.5
80331 Munich, Germany
Tel. 089-2366-21-30
Fax 089-260-4009

International Tourism Network (ITN)
Room 802, Namkyung Bldg. 8-2
Samsung-Dong Kangnam-Ku
Seoul, Korea
Tel. 02-3445-9283
Fax 02-3445-9285

You'll also found a bounty of information on the Internet about Las Vegas attractions, hotels, and shows. The official Las Vegas Convention and Visitors Authority site is: *www.lasvegas24hours.com.*

We've also provided an appendix of additional Internet sites at the end of this book. See Appendix B for a rundown of the many excellent web sites that can provide you with up-to-date information on show times, attraction prices, and more.

ARRIVALS & DEPARTURES

Travel agents offer a (usually) free service, making hotel and air reservations and issuing airline tickets. They can shop around for the lowest rate for you and often know about sales that aren't known to the general public.

Stop by a travel agency and talk to an agent during an off-peak time, usually early morning or mid-day. Tell him or her your likes and dislikes and your budget range. The agent can help you start to narrow your choices to a few resorts. Pick up some brochures, head home, and talk over the choices with your family.

Now the fun part: doing some research. Rent some travel videos. Look at some guidebooks and travel magazines. Get on the Internet and check out some travel forums for other people's views. Talk about your options.

When you have your minds made up – or at least narrowed down – return to the travel agent for some help. If it's a large office, ask for the agent who specializes in Las Vegas.

Now the agent can assist you with the nitty-gritty of the travel task: making your reservations. Often you'll need to put down a deposit on reservations or packages. This deposit may be non-refundable so make sure that you have made your final selection both in terms of resort and travel dates.

By Commercial Air

The first many travelers see of Las Vegas is the **Las Vegas McCarran International Airport** *(www.mccarran.com)*, located one mile from the Strip. Coming in at night to this airport provides one of the best aerial views in the world; you'll have a bird's eye view of the neon and glitter that makes this city what it is.

The airport is served by numerous carriers, both scheduled and charter flights from around the globe.

Scheduled Carriers include:

Air Canada
www.aircanada.ca
Tel. 800/776-3000

Alaska Airlines
www.alaskaair.com
Tel. 800/426-0333

Allegiant Air
www.allegiant-air.com
Tel. 877/202-6444

America West
www.americawest.com
Tel. 800/2 FLY AWA

American Airlines
www.aa.com
Tel. 800/433-7300

American Trans Air
www.ata.com
Tel. 800/I-FLY-ATA

COMAIR
www.fly-comair.com
Tel. 800/I-FLY-ATA

Continental Airlines
www.continental.com
Tel. 800/525-0280

Delta Airlines
www.delta-air.com
Tel. 800/221-1212

Frontier
www.flyfrontier.com
Tel. 800/432-1359

Hawaiian
www.hawaiianair.com
Tel. 800/367-5320

Japan Airlines
www.jal.co.jp/english/index_e.html
Tel. 800/525-3663

Legend Airlines
www.legendairlines.com
Tel. 800/452-2022

National Airlines
www.nationalairlines.com
Tel. 888/757-5387

Northwest Airlines
www.nwa.com
Tel. 800/225-2525

Southwest Airlines
www.southwest.com
Tel. 800/I-FLY-SWA

Sun Country
www.suncountry.com
Tel. 800/752-1218

Sunrise Airlines
www.sunriseair.net
Tel. 800/I-FLY-ATA

TWA
www.twa.com
Tel. 800/221-2000

United Airlines
www.ual.com
Tel. 800/241-6522

United Express
www.ual.com/airline/Our_Services/express.asp
Tel. 800/453-9417

US Airways

www.usairways.com
Tel. 800/428-4322

By Charter Air

Las Vegas is also served by many charter companies. These carriers may just run during certain times of the year or on certain days of the week, but rates are often low. Some are booked only through travel agents so they don't have reservation numbers, but all have websites (and a few can be booked directly online).

If you've got some flexibility in your plans, it can be worth it to check out charter carriers like these:

Aero Mexico

www.aeromexico.com
Tel. 800/AEROMEX

Air Canada

www.aircanada.ca
Tel. 800/776-3000

Air France

www.airfrance.fr
Tel. 800/237-2747

Air Trans AT

www.transat.com

Allegiant Air

www.allegiant-air.com
Tel. 559/454-7730 or 877/202/6444

American Trans Air
www.ata.com
Tel. 800/I-FLY-ATA

Canada 3000
www.Canada3000.ca
Tel. 888/CAN3000

Champion Air
www.championair.com

Condor Flugdienst
www.condor.de

Eagle/Scenic
www.scenic.com
Tel. 800/638-3330

Mexicana
www.mexicana.com.mx
Tel. 800/531-7921

If you notice that the airport is busy, you're right. McCarran International Airport sees nearly 34 million passengers a year, up over 11% from just the year before.

Package Deals

Several airlines offer package deals that provide a complete vacation: room, transfers, air. Is this cheaper than putting a package together on your own? Usually. Check it out for yourself by calling the hotel reservation numbers, asking for their room rate and adding it to the cost of an airline ticket. You'll generally see a substantial savings, since, after all, the airlines are buying rooms in bulk and therefore have much more purchasing power than an ordinary consumer.

Some travelers worry about the term "package," imagining a trip where they'll be herded on a tour bus with a plane full of tourists. Have no fear. Some packages include the services of a greeter at the airport who will welcome you and show you the way to the transfer bus to your hotel, but beyond that you're on your own. If you want to rent a car and explore, go to it.

Packages are also offered by charter airlines, carriers that offer service at lower cost, usually with few frills. (Often only one class of service is available, seat assignments are given only at check-in, and carry on allowances may be only one bag per passenger due to an increased number of seats onboard.) If you don't want the package vacation, some of these charters also sell "air-only," just the airline tickets themselves.

You'll find some good packages for Las Vegas that include air and accommodations. Some packages, however, are only offered for guests over age 21. The reason: if you're not over 21, you're not a potential gambler. These airlines, however, offer good packages for the whole family:

American Express Vacations
Tel. 800/241-1700

AA FlyAway Vacations
Tel. 800/321-2121

America West Vacations
Tel. 800/356-6611

HELP YOUR KIDS ENJOY FLYING

• *Talk to you kids about flying, from the sounds they'll hear to the layout of the plane and the behavior that will be expected of them.*

• *Book seat assignments early so the family sits together. (If you're flying on a charter carrier that doesn't pre-assign seats, get to the airport extra early to ensure that your group will stay together.)*

• *Order special kid's meals from the airline reservation number at least a day in advance. Special meals, available at no extra charge, contain kid favorites and also help make children feel part of the trip.*

• *Minimize your luggage. You'll travel lighter (remember the "lug" in luggage!) and check-in will be faster.*

• *Arrive at the airport early. Check in for flights is 1-1/2 hours before departure at most airports.*

• *Consider preboarding if you want to get seated before the mad dash onto the plane begins. However, if your child is restless, this will only add to total time on the ground before takeoff.*

• *Bring bottles and pacifiers for young children to ease the pressure on the inner ear during take offs and landings. For older children, bring chewing gum.*

• *Pack some special activities in a secret "goody bag" or two you keep out the child's hands until the trip is underway.*

• *Bring extra batteries for older children's electronic games and headsets.*

Delta Dream Vacations
Tel. 800/872-7786

Southwest Airlines Vacations
Tel. 800/423-5683

United Airlines Vacations
Tel. 800/328-6877

US Airways Vacations
Tel. 800/455-0123

Frequent Flier Programs

When you purchase your airline ticket, sign up for the frequent flyer program. Also, check to see if your hotel or rental car company is part of the frequent flyer program. Today you can earn mileage in many ways other than flying. Long distance companies, credit card companies, dining programs, and others offer miles, sometimes as many as five for every dollar spent.

And what's in it for you? With enough miles, you'll soon be earning a frequent flyer pass for a free ticket. What better way to head back to Las Vegas!

Arriving by Car

Las Vegas is an easy destination to reach by car, thanks to the many highways in every direction. Here's a quick rundown of roads leading to the neon city:

- I-15 from San Diego
- I-40 from Flagstaff to US Hwy. 95, then north to Boulder City
- I-15 south from Salt Lake City (a route that travels past many national parks)

GETTING AROUND TOWN

City Layout

The **Strip** is a stretch of Las Vegas Boulevard South that runs between Sahara Avenue and Russell Road. This is ground-zero for the latest hotel boom; here's where you'll find all the hot resort hotels.

Downtown is the older section of Las Vegas, an area that's now sporting a fresher look thanks to the Fremont Street Experience (see more about it in the "Do We Have to Go to Bed?" chapter) and recent renovations. Downtown is the area around the intersection of Fremont Street and Main Street; it's near the northern portion of Las Vegas Boulevard South.

Getting from the Airport to Your Hotel

You'll got several choices once you land: rent a car, grab an airport shuttle, hop the hotel shuttle (an option for only a few hotels), or grab a taxi.

Hotels that offer airport-pickup for their guests include the Frontier and Westward Ho. Check with other hotels when you make your reservation, but don't hold your breath.

These companies offer mini-buses and service to downtown and strip hotels:

Bell Trans
Tel. 702/739-7990
You can arrange a ride for $3.75 per person to the Strip or $5 to downtown hotels with this company.

Gray Line
Tel. 702/739-5700
Gray Line offers transfers to the Strip for $4.40 per person (or $7.70 round trip), or $5.50 to downtown hotels ($9.90 round trip).

Ray and Ross Airport Express
Tel. 702/261-3230
This company offers transfers to the Strip for $4 ($7 round trip), downtown for $5 ($9 round trip).

Renting a Car

OK, the hotel's not going to pick you up and you don't want to take a shuttle. Time to look at the rental cars.

First, let us give you a little warning. Traffic here is horrendous. Maybe it's because some of the drivers are not so happy with the day's bets, maybe it's the incredible amount of construction constantly underway, maybe it's the high number of new residents who relocate to Las Vegas every day. Whatever the reason, Las Vegas is not a destination for sissy drivers. That said, you can save money renting a car. Cabs here aren't cheap and walking from place to place will have you seeing more than one mirage along the Strip.

You'll find rental cars available from these agencies:

Advantage
Tel. 800/877-5500
www.arac.com

Alamo
Tel. 800/327-9633
www.goalamo.com

Avis
Tel. 800/331-1212
www.avis.com

Budget
Tel. 800/527-0700
www.budgetrentalcar.com

Dollar
Tel. 800/800-4000
www.dollarcar.com

Enterprise
Tel. 800/325-8007
www.pickenterprise.com

TIP TIPS

Tipping is such a part of Las Vegas life it's received its own name: toke. A toke or tip can be paid out for everything from restaurant service to a better seat at a shows. Here's a sample of tokes you should expect to pay:

Bellmen: *$1 per bag*

Hotel maids: *$2 per day (paid at the end of your stay)*

Maitre 'd in showroom: *$5-$20*

Pool attendants: *$1*

Servers in showroom: *$5-$10 for non-dinner show, 15% for dinner show*

Taxi drivers: *$1-$2*

Tour guides: *$1-$2 per person*

Valet parkers: *$1*

Waiters/waitresses: *15% of bill*

Hertz
Tel. 800/654-3131
www.hertz.com

National
Tel. 800/CAR-RENT
www.nationalcar.com

Payless
Tel. 800/PAYLESS
www.paylesscar.com

Thrifty
Tel. 800/367-2277
www.thrifty.com

Public Transportation

Las Vegas has several shuttle systems that will whisk you and your family to the city attractions and all the major hotels. Here are your choices:

Strip Trolley. For this ride, you'll need exact change of $1.30. The trolley runs every day from 9:30am to 2am, about every 20 minutes. The trolleys run up and down the Strip from the Sahara to the Luxor, stopping in front of each major hotel along the way. A good way to avoid the crush of traffic and the hassle of parking in this congested area!

Monorails and Trams. Hey, it's a free ride! Wee...it's just like Disneyland. Yes, you penny-pinching parents of young visitors may just be able to sell this one as a genuine ride. Save a few steps with a ride on these:

• Bally's to MGM Grand Monorail
• Luxor to Excalibur Monorail
• Mirage to Treasure Island Tram
• Mirage to Caesars Palace People Mover

Hotel Shuttles. You'll also find that many hotels run free shuttles to other hotels. Here's a rundown of these free options:

• Barbary Coast to Gold Coast
• California Hotel to Sam's Town
• Fiesta to Fashion Show Mall
• Fremont to Sam's Town
• Hard Rock Cafe to Fashion Show Mall
• Hard Rock Cafe to MGM Grand
• Palace Station to Texas Station
• Rio Suites to Fashion Show Mall

- Rio Suites to MGM Grand
- Rio Suites to Stardust
- Sam's Town to California Hotel
- Silverton to Fashion Show Mall
- Stardust to Sam's Town

2. WHERE ARE WE?

TOURS OF LAS VEGAS & VICINITY

Guided tours are a great way to get a quick feel for a destination. No, you won't feel like a nerd, packed on a bus with a bunch of camera-wearing tourists ... OK, you might, but you'll get over that after just a few minutes. Remember, just about everyone in Las Vegas either is a tourist or first came to the city as a tourist! For their price, tours are a good bargain to get the most out of your stay and to see sights both in the city and outside the city limits.

GROUND TOURS OF LAS VEGAS

You'll find several operators who offer bus tours of Las Vegas and the surrounding regions. Call these operators for more information:

Gray Line Tours
4020 E. Lone Mountain Rd.
Las Vegas, NV 89031
Tel. 702/384-1234
Toll Free 800/634-6579
Fax 702/632-2118
www.grayline.com

Gray Line offers several city tours. The **Neon and Lights tour** spans 3-1/2 hours and showcases the highlights of the Strip as well as the Fremont Street Experience. The tour departs at 6:30 nightly; the price is $28 for adults and $26 for children ages 5-11.

The **Glitter City Tour** spans about three hours and showcases the names that made Las Vegas famous, from Bugsy Siegal to Howard Hughes. The tour includes Wedding Chapel Row and the Fremont Street Experience. This tour is offered twice daily at 8:30 am and 1pm; the cost is $25 for adults and $21 for children ages 5-11.

Mountain West Travel, LV

2549 New Morning Ave.
Henderson, NV 89012
Tel. 702/270-2704
Fax 702/270-2705

This tour operator offers driving tours of the city for bilingual clients and also takes groups to the nearby national parks. They also provide hotel pickup.

Nevada Tours and Travel

795 E. Tropicana Ave., 1st Floor
Las Vegas, NV 89119
Tel. 702/895-8873
Toll Free 888/413-7184
Fax 702/895-9251
www.nevadacharter.com

This operator has a variety of local tours of the city. The Premier Night Tour ($29) operates Tuesday, Thursday, Friday and Saturday nights and takes visitors on a five hour look at the city, from the Mirage Volcano to Treasure Island's pirate battle to

Bellagio's fountains to the Fremont Street Experience. The trip concludes with a stop at the Hard Rock Cafe.

GROUND TOURS OUTSIDE LAS VEGAS

Creative Adventures

P.O. Box 94043
Las Vegas, NV 89193-4043
Tel. 702/361-5565
Fax 702/893-2061

How about a tour by a professional guide who's also a story-teller? Sign up for one of these area tours and that's just what you'll get, with a guide that weaves the history and richness of the region into every tour.

Drive-Yourself Tours

8170 S. Eastern Avenue #4-278
Las Vegas, NV 89123
Tel. 702/565-8761
Fax 702/565-5786
www.drive-yourselftours.com

We like the idea of these tours: no tour guide, no fellow travelers, just you, your car and your tape player. These tours are a series of self-guided audio cassettes with maps that take you to local attractions.

Grand Canyon Tour Company

4894 Lone Mountain Rd #137
Las Vegas, NV 89130
Tel. 702/655-6060
Toll Free 800/2-CANYON
Fax 702/655-6323
www.grandcanyontourcompany.com

How about a tour of Grand Canyon or Hoover Dam? This company has a variety of packages ranging from airplane and helicopter tours to river rafting and bus tours.

Gray Line Tours
4020 E. Lone Mountain Rd.
Las Vegas, NV 89031
Tel. 702/384-1234
Toll Free 800/634-6579
Fax 702/632-2118
www.grayline.com

We've traveled with Gray Line Tours many times and always enjoyed the professional attitude and fun tours provided by this company.

One interesting area tour this company offers is the 1800s Old West Cowboy Tour. The trip includes Red Rock Canyon as well as Bonnie Springs and some old mining towns. This tour, nearly four hours, departs at 8:30am and 1:30pm daily; the price is $29 for adults and $25 for children 5-11.

Another tour is the Grand Canyon Indian Country Tour, where travelers learn about the history of the Las Vegas Valley. The tour stops at the Hualapai Indian Reservation and a Native American guide takes the tour for a look at Grand Cayon. The trip includes a native barbecue lunch. This tour takes 10 hours and departs at 7:30am daily; the cost is $119 for adults, $109 for children ages 5-11.

Nevada Tours and Travel
795 E. Tropicana Ave., 1st Floor
Las Vegas, NV 89119
Tel. 702/895-8873

Toll Free 888/413-7184
Fax 702/895-9251
www.nevadacharter.com

This company has a mini-Hoover Dam Mini Tour on Monday-Saturday ($24). The half-day tour travels to the dam and the Hoover Dam Visitor's Center, ending with a stop at the Ethel M Chocolate Factory. The Deluxe Hoover Dam Tour ($34) takes a seven-hour look at Hoover Dam and visitor's center, stopping at a hotel for a buffet lunch then continuing to Ethel M Chocolate Factory.

Nevada Zoological Foundation Desert Eco-Tours

1775 N. Rancho Dr.
Las Vegas, NV 89106
Tel. 702/647-4685
www.lvrj.com/communitylink/zoo

Want to learn more about the desert? These half and full-day tours provide a fun way for families to learn more about the desert region. If you've got a rock hunter in the family or anyone interested in ghost towns, these tours are great. Tours include hotel pick-up and an orientation to acquaint you with the rocks and wildlife you'll see along the trip.

Both private and bus tours are offered. They've got a variety of tours including gemstone collecting, historic mining, ghost towns, "Area 51" (watch out for those aliens!), and more.

Quality Tours

2961 Industrial Rd., Suite #47
Las Vegas, NV 89109
Tel. 702/631-2292
www.qtlv.com

This operator offers daytrips to Grand Canyon, Hoover Dam, Lake Mead, and Laughlin by plane or bus.

FLIGHTSEEING TOURS TO GRAND CANYON

Several tour companies offer tour options in the air. These are, as you might expect, expensive but they do offer a unique and really memorable way to see the region and points beyond.

Several companies offer guided flightseeing tours to the Grand Canyon. Yes, you can take a quick buzz from Las Vegas to the Grand Canyon and doing it by plane is just about the only way to see this natural wonder without adding several days onto your stay. Flightseeing companies to Grand Canyon include:

Air Nevada Airlines, *Tel. 702/736-3599 or 800/255-7474, Fax 702/896-2906, E-mail airvegas@skylink.net*, offers flightseeing tour packages that include lunch, the guide's services, and hotel transfers.

Air Vegas Airlines, *Tel. 702/736-3599 or 800/255-7474, Fax 702/896-2906*, offers tours to Grand Canyon and includes hotel transfers.

Eagle Canyon Airlines, *Tel. 702/736-3333 or 800/446-4584, Fax 702/895-7824, www.eagleair.com*, has tours available in several languages.

HeliUSA, *Tel. 702/736-8787, Fax 702/735-0835, www.heliusa.com*, offers helicopter tours of Grand Canyon.

Lake Mead Air, *Tel. 702/293-1848*, offers Grand Canyon flights and charters.

Scenic Airlines, Tel. *707-638-3300, www.scenic.com,* offers flightseeing tours of the Grand Canyon (as well as trips to Monument Valley and Bryce Canyon).

FLIGHTSEEING TOURS OF LAS VEGAS

There's no better time to see Las Vegas than when the lights begin to come up and that's when **Las Vegas Airship Tours**, *Tel. 877/LV-BLIMP,* takes a look at the city. This is really a unique ride: you board a nine-passenger blimp for a view of the Strip, starting at sunset.

Another option is a helicopter tour of the city with **Nevada Tours and Travel**, *Tel. 702/895-8873, Toll Free 888/413-7184, Fax 702/895-9251, www.nevadacharter.com.* For $65, this nightly tour takes travelers high over the Strip for an unforgettable view of the lights.

3. WHY IS THERE A VOLCANO ON THIS STREET?

A LOOK AT THE ONE-OF-KIND LAS VEGAS STRIP

Las Vegas has taken theme concepts to new heights and produced a fantasyland like no other place on earth. Here you can visit ancient Egypt, King Arthur's Court, a tropical rainforest, Venice, New York, Paris, Rio's Carnaval, and more – without ever spending a dime.

The new level of theme casino hotels began with the construction of The Mirage. This dynamo brought to the Strip a "volcano," a rainforest and – even more important – a whole new vitality. Soon the theme concept was proclaimed a Royal Flush and, in no time, occupancy rates rose right along with the number of hotel rooms – making Las Vegas definitely a Full House.

Throughout this book, you'll find features of the hotel resorts included and examined in different chapters. We'll look at the hotel accommodations themselves in "Which One is My Room?" We'll cover the attractions – from arcades to jousting – in "What Are We Doing Next?" Family-friendly restaurants are covered in

"What's for Dinner?" and shows at hotel-casinos are included in "Do We Have to Go to Bed Yet?"

But in this section, we're going to give you the highlights of the best themed casino hotels. You may not be a guest at these properties, but you'll want to make time to drop by, have a look around, and enjoy some of the globe's most unique hotels.

While hotels in other cities may seem like the realm of guests only, in Las Vegas the welcome mat is definitely out for all. Come by, have fun, and enjoy the theme hotels, even if you're staying in a budget motel miles away.

The distance from hotel to hotel can be deceiving. When you visit a hotel, you very likely may want to take in all its features – from rides to shows to dining.

In this chapter, we'll take you down the Strip geographically, north to south. Buckle your seat belts, we're cruisin' the Strip!

SOUTH OF MAIN STREET

The northernmost hotel we'll be covering on the Strip is the **Stratosphere**. Don't worry about that address, just look up. This mega-building is the Stratosphere Tower, the tallest freestanding observation tower in the US and the tallest building west of the Mississippi River. For the best view of the city, you'll want to buzz up to the **Pepsi Cola Observation Decks**. Daredevils in the group will want to try the **Big Shot** and the **High Roller**, two of the wildest rides in the nation.

For more on those attractions, see "What Are We Doing Next?" chapter later in this book.

SOUTH OF SAHARA AVENUE

This block is the capital of the Strip as far as families are concerned. In one block, you'll find the non-stop (and free!) circus at Circus Circus, the hotel's **Adventure Dome theme park, Wet 'n Wild Water Park**, and more. We're just giving you a quick tease of the attractions found at each resort in this section; for more details on the attractions, see the chapter "What Are We Doing Next?" later in this book. For more on the hotels themselves, see the "Which One is My Room?" chapter.

Circus Circus is ground zero for the school age crowd. Circus Circus is the top hotel for families in the city thanks to its circus, **Adventuredome** theme park, and general kids' theme. With it's big top exterior, there's no missing this kids' mega-plex.

Across the street from Circus Circus stands the **Sahara**. This hotel is undergoing a major renovation and is home to **Sahara Speedworld**, a dream come true for arcade lovers and those in search of 3-D action, as well as Speed – The Ride, a real screamer of a rollercoaster.

South of Sahara lies **Wet 'n Wild**. This park calls out like a fire engine on a hot Vegas afternoon, with rides of all speeds, from hair-raising (if you can raise wet hair) to relaxing. They've got a special kids' section that's a sure hit with the smallest travelers.

SOUTH OF DESERT INN ROAD

Keep on cruising south on Las Vegas Boulevard, cross Desert Inn Road, and you'll reach a fairly short (by Vegas standards) block that's the home of the **Fashion Show Mall**. Many trolleys depart from this central point; you'll also find plenty of typical mall shopping here (more on that in "What Can I Buy?")

SOUTH OF SPRING MOUNTAIN ROAD

This is a major block, the home of several "must see" theme casinos. Just south of Spring Mountain Road is **Treasure Island**. From its **pirate battle** waged outside to its high-tech video arcade indoors, this resort's a favorite with families.

Across the street from Treasure Island stands the new **Venetian**. With its elegant, romantic theme, the Venetian's not a property aimed at children but it is home to the **gondola rides**, a fun way to take a quick trip to Italy for even a few minutes.

Just south of Treasure Island lies **The Mirage**. With its South Sea tropical theme, The Mirage is another favorite with families and one of our personal favorites. Outside, you can't miss the **volcano**, one of the highlights of the Strip. You'll ride to the Mirage on a moving sidewalk to a cacophony of jungle sounds. From the minute you enter the front doors, you're greeted by the feel and sound of the **rainforest**, from tropical plants to a mega-aquarium at check-in. Inside, Royal Siberian white tigers lounge around their **habitat**, waiting for their nightly performance in the Siegfried and Roy show. In the hotel, you'll wind your way past an indoor jungle, through a casino of ringing slot machines, and out to the **Dolphin Habitat**. This $14 million pool is home to Atlantic bottle-nose dolphins who delight visitors of all ages with their aquatic antics.

Across the street from The Mirage lies **Harrah's**. This casino hotel is aimed at adults but families will enjoy the **Carnaval Court**, an outdoor area with the feel of a street fair, complete with hot dog vendors and, during the spring and summer months, live entertainment.

South of Harrah's lies the **Imperial Palace**. This Asian-themed hotel is home to an extensive **auto collection**, as well as the **Legends**

in Concert impersonator's show and **Hawaiian Hot Luau** from April through October.

South of the Imperial Palace lies the **Flamingo Hilton**. This hotel is where Las Vegas as we know it all began in 1946. The original hotel built by Bugsy Siegel, the Flamingo is home to, appropriately enough, the **Flamingo Habitat**, filled with the colorful birds.

Crossing back across Las Vegas Boulevard, you'll find the **Forum Shops** at Caesars Palace. Yes, this exclusive shopping center is home to many shops, but, of special interest to families, it's also home to the free **Fountain Show**, the **Lost City of Atlantis**, and the **Cinema Ride**, all motion simulation rides.

Just south of the Forum Shops is **Caesars Palace**. This luxurious hotel is aimed at adults, but families – until recently – would have found several fun features. Now families will still enjoy a look at the Roman theme (hey, is that Cleopatra over there?).

SOUTH OF FLAMINGO ROAD

Head on across Flamingo Road and you'll reach the **Bellagio**. This really is an adults' casino hotel – so much so that children are not permitted in the property unless they're guests. You don't need to enter the hotel, though, to enjoy the **Bellagio Fountains**, a beautiful display of choreographed fountains that shoot over 240 feet in the air.

Across from Bellagio is **Bally's**. This hotel casino also has an adult atmosphere, although children are welcome. There's a monorail here to take you to the MGM.

South of Bally's is **Paris**. Can't find it, you say? Just look for the Eiffel Tower. Yep, this hotel sports a half-size replica of the **Eiffel Tower**, where a ride offers a speactacular view of the city.

South of Paris is **Aladdin**. Not yet open at press time, this hotel will sport a Middle Eastern theme that promises to be fun.

Continue on down Las Vegas Boulevard (this is a huge block). Next you'll reach the **MGM Grand**. With its signature lions out front, you'll easily recognize this mega-hotel. The hotel is home to **MGM Grand Adventures**, a theme park that's a fun stop for families.

Across from the MGM Grand stands **New York New York**. Yes, it's the skyline of New York atop this building...complete with the **Manhattan Express roller coaster** as well.

SOUTH OF TROPICANA AVENUE

Continue south on the Strip across Tropicana Avenue and you'll reach **Excalibur**. With its King Arthur theme, this grand hotel is easy to spot with its white turrets and drawbridge. In front of the hotel, knights battle for victory in the free **Dragon Battle** (complete with a fire-breathing dragon, of course). The hotel is also home to **Magic Motion Rides**, simulated motion rides that give film viewers the sensation of moving along with the action.

South of Excalibur lies **Luxor**, a tribute to ancient Egypt as only Las Vegas could do it. This pyramid-shaped hotel is home to a full-size replica of King Tut's tomb, a real winner with kids.

Across from Luxor is **Tropicana**. A long-time favorite on the Strip, this hotel sports, you guessed it, a tropical theme. They've got a five-acre **swimming area/water park** as well as a **Wildlife Walk** filled with tropical birds.

4. WHICH ONE IS MY ROOM?

GREAT PLACES TO STAY WITH KIDS

Remember all those tales of cheap rooms throughout Las Vegas? Well, times have changed. You will still find inexpensive rooms compared to other cities, but don't look for $19 rooms at most properties. With demand higher than ever (a 95% occupancy rate isn't uncommon on many weekends), prices have risen, although good deals still can be found. The key is to make your reservation in advance. The city is home to over 120,000 hotel rooms but they are in demand.

You won't find a single reservation service that handles all Las Vegas properties, but you can call the **Las Vegas Convention and Visitors Authority** (LVCVA), *Tel. 702/386-0770 or 800/332-5333*, to check on availability at many properties. Call the office from Monday through Saturday between 7am and 7pm or Sunday from 8:30am to 6pm. Another option is to call the hotels directly. We've included toll-free reservation numbers and direct hotel lines in these listings, as well as internet addresses whenever available. Many hotels take reservations directly over the Internet (and some offer specials on their Web sites not available through travel agents).

In selecting a hotel, you want to look for kid-friendly features. Some casino hotels are really focused primarily on the casino, and that doesn't leave kids much to do. We've pointed out which hotels offer attractions, good swimming pools, restaurants with kids' menus, and other assets that will make the kids feel like part of the vacation, not just little travelers to be shuttled at warp speed through the casino (don't stop!) on the way to the elevators.

But you will see that we've included all the major hotels in Las Vegas in this chapter. Why? In an ideal world, we know that you'd pick the most kid-friendly properties for your family vacation. But we also know that, realistically speaking, there are other factors involved. You may be in Las Vegas for a convention and not have a choice of hotels. You may be taking the package with the best price and have very little choice of hotels. We've given you the pros and cons of the hotels that aren't really designed for families (although families do make up part of the guest list at all these properties, whether the management likes it or not).

First, a look at the hotels we really recommend as kid-friendly. If you've got a choice, look at these selections first. After this, we'll cover other properties, both hotels and motels in Las Vegas. If you're traveling with teens, you may find that some of the hotels we didn't select as kid-friendly will be just perfect for older children, and we've given you tips in selecting those properties as well.

HOTEL PRICES IN THIS BOOK

We've used the following designations for hotel prices:

$$$: over $150 per night
$$: $75-$150
$: under $75 per night

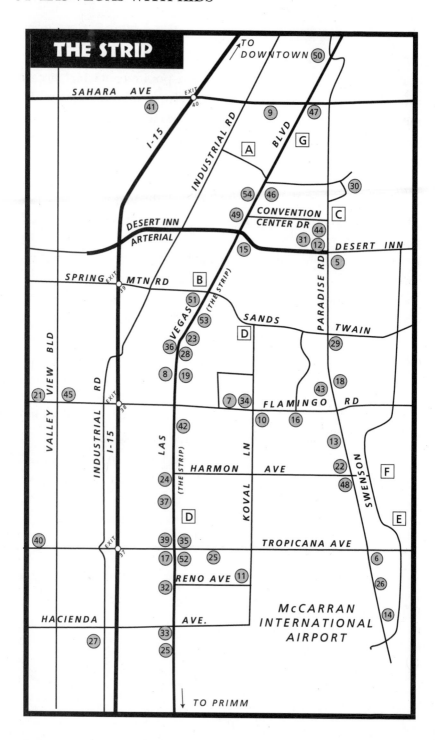

1. Alexis Park
2. Bally's
3. Barbary Coast
4. Bellagio
5. Best Western Mardi Gras
6. Best Western McCarran
7. Bourbon Street
8. Caesars Palace
9. Circus Circus
10. Comfort Inn (Central)
11. Comfort Inn South
12. Courtyard by Marriott
13. Crowne Plaza Holiday Inn
14. Days Inn Airport
15. Desert Inn
16. Emerald Springs Holiday Inn
17. Excalibur
18. Fairfield Inn
19. Flamingo Hilton
20. Four Seasons
21. Gold Coast
22. Hard Rock Hotel
23. Harrah's
24. Holiday Inn Boardwalk
25. Hotel San Remo
26. Howard Johnson's Airport
27. Howard Johnson's Plaza
28. Imperial Palace
29. La Quinta Inn Convention Center
30. Las Vegas Hilton
31. Las Vegas Marriott Suites
32. Luxor
33. Mandalay Bay
34. Maxim
35. MGM Grand
36. Mirage
37. Monte Carlo
38. Motel 6 at Tropicana
39. New York, New York
40. Orleans
41. Palace Station
42. Paris
43. Residence Inn by Marriott

44. Residence Inn by Marriott
45. Rio
46. Riviera
47. Sahara
48. St. Tropez
49. Stardust
50. Stratosphere
51. Treasure Island
52. Tropicana
53. Venetian
54. Westward Ho

A. Adventure Dome at
      Circus Circus
B. Fashion Show Mall
C. Las Vegas Convention
      Center
D. MGM Grand Adventures
E. Thomas & Mack Center
F. UNLV
G. Wet 'n' Wild

Pricing of Las Vegas hotels is a hard thing to pin down. All hotels have a variety of rates, starting with the "rack rate," the highest rate that's given over the phone with no discounts or specials. From there, hotels have a complex system of pricing, depending on the month, the day of the week, the cycle of the moon, no one knows for sure.

In Las Vegas, that pricing system is even more complicated. We've seen $150 rooms priced at $39 on certain days. However, what we've listed here is the average price on a given day. You'll find prices higher on holidays, weekends, and whenever there's a mega-convention in hotel. Prices are lowest mid-week.

We've used these general designations rather than specific prices because there are so many prices available at any given point. These designations will give you a ballpark figure of what to expect and how hotels rate in relation to each other.

You'll also find that there are as many prices as there are chips on a blackjack table. If at first you don't get the price you want, try, try again. Keep calling, be somewhat flexible with days, and you very well might get a better deal.

The following hotels have been selected as the best Las Vegas has to offer families. Here you'll find family-friendly staffs, special attractions aimed at youngsters, and a fun atmosphere where your family will feel comfortable. For more on the hotel's attractions, see the "What Are We Doing Next?" chapter later in this book.

THE BEST FAMILY-FRIENDLY HOTELS
CIRCUS CIRCUS

2880 Las Vegas Boulevard South, Tel. 702/734-0410 or 800/634-3450, Fax 702/734-0410, www.circuscircus.com.

$49.00   Thurs/Fri   5th/6th
                          49.00 $109.00

Rates: *$$*
Amenities: *RV park, casino, wedding chapel, salon*
Family-friendly features: *circus, theme park, arcade*

If you've got young children, Circus Circus is the number one choice. From its decor to its entertainment, the focus is on family fun.

The hotel includes a bustling casino, but this resort has many features aimed at the under-21 and the non-gambling set. The hotel has over 3700 guest rooms, each considered oversized at 460 square feet; all rooms have air conditioning, color TV with cable and pay channels, 24-hour room service, and more.

Adjacent to the resort lies Circusland RV Park, a 384-space campground with its own playground and arcade.

EXCALIBUR

3850 Las Vegas Boulevard South, Tel. 702/597-7777 or 800/937-7777, Fax 702/597-7040, www.excalibur-casino.com.

Rates: *$$-$$$*
Amenities: *six restaurants, casino*
Family-friendly features: *two swimming pools, Dragon Battle, Magic Motion Rides, play area, WCW Nitro Grill, court jesters, Tournament of Kings dinner show, food court*

This 4008-room hotel was one of the first in Las Vegas to take a theme and run with it. As soon as you see its white towers, drawbridge, and moat, you know you're somewhere special. The King Arthur theme is carried through in everything from its restaurants to its entertainment.

You'll walk up a drawbridge into this castle-like hotel, where jugglers, knights in armor, and costumed minstrels stroll around in a very un-casino like atmosphere. The first floor of the hotel is specially designed for children, with craft booths, medieval games, and two popular magic motion machines. The third floor contains the Medieval Village, with theme restaurants and shops that sell everything from magic wands to toy swords.

Inside, the guest rooms each have air conditioning, color TV with pay channels, 24-hour room service, and more.

HOLIDAY INN BOARDWALK

3750 Las Vegas Boulevard South, Tel. 702/735-1167 or 800/465-4329, Fax 702/739-8152, www.hiboardwalk.com.

Rates: *$-$$*
Amenities: *casino, tour desk, non-smoking rooms, coffee shop, restaurant, cable TV, coffee makers, irons, room service, three dining facilities, 24-hour food service, shops, bell service, valet service, tour desk, fitness room, car rental, free parking garage*
Family-friendly features: *Location across from MGM Grand Adventures theme park, two pools*

They call this 600-room hotel "the Coney Island of Las Vegas" and with a look at its facade, it's easy to see why. With its good location across from MGM, the hotel also has plenty of attractions for families in its own right.

The show here is **"The Dream King,"** *www.dreamking.com*, a tribute to (you guessed it) Elvis. Kids under 12 are free for the show.

Dining here is also kid-friendly. The Caffe Boardwalk is the main dining room and is open daily for breakfast, lunch and dinner. The Deli is open 24 hours and has plenty of kid favorites like Coney Island hot dogs. The Surf Buffet is also open 24 hours and has American food as well as Italian, Mexican, and Asian specialties, all enjoyed in a beach-themed eatery. If the kids have a sweet tooth (what do we mean "if"?), stop by Coney Island Ice Cream parlor for a scoop and grab an iced coffee, mocha, or specialty coffee drink for yourself.

Rates at this property are very good, especially considering its location. We recently saw a $35 per night special for particular dates. Don't look for that special at just any time, but you will find good rates here most days.

LUXOR

3900 Las Vegas Boulevard South, Tel. 702/262-4000 or 800/288-1000, Fax 702/262-4452, www.luxor.com.

Rates: *$$*
Amenities: *casino, spa, 24-hour room service, Jacuzzi suites*
Family-Friendly Features: *IMAX theater, replica of King Tut's Tomb, Games of the Gods arcade, pool*

Luxor is housed in a truly royal pyramid that soars 350 feet in the air. The 36-story building contains the world's largest atrium.

At night, it's easy to find the Luxor – just look up. From the pinnacle of the pyramid shines the brightest beam of light in the world. It is produced by 45 Xenon lights and projects a beam that you could read a newspaper by even 10 miles in space. This 4400-room hotel offers well-appointed rooms, all with a view of the Strip, the mountains, or the large pool.

MGM GRAND HOTEL AND CASINO

3799 Las Vegas Boulevard South, 800/929-1111 or 702/891-7777, www.mgmgrand.com.

Rates: *$$-$$$*
Amenities: *casino, nine room styles, spa suites, 16 restaurants*
Family-Friendly **Features**: *MGM Grand Adventures theme park, supervised children's program*

This hotel really is grand: 5,034 rooms worth. Sporting an MGM movie theme, you'll recognize the hotel by its jumbo golden lions at the front entrance. Inside, the theme continues with each room decorated in a classic style with black and white marble bathrooms.

This hotel is spread out across four 30-story towers (so large, in fact, that we almost got lost on our first stay here). There are nine categories of rooms, starting with the Deluxe Rooms in the Grand Tower. These are all 446 square feet and are well appointed.

FUN FACTS ABOUT THE MGM GRAND

• *This hotel has 18,000 doors (enough to outfit 1,600 three-bedroom homes!)*
• *If all the beds in this hotel were stacked on top of each other, the pile would be 10 times taller than the Empire State Building.*
• *The core of central elevators is the size of a major downtown skyscraper.*
• *Don't worry about summer heat here – the hotel has 18,000 tons of air conditioning equipment (enough for a town of 5500 houses).*
• *It would take 13 years and 8 months for a person to sleep one night in every room in this hotel.*
• *Over 18 million eggs are cooked at this hotel every year.*

TREASURE ISLAND

3300 Las Vegas Boulevard South, Tel. 702/894-7111 or 800/944-7444, Fax 702/894-7446, www.treasureisland.com.

Rates: *$$-$$$*
Amenities: *casino, high speed internet access in some rooms*
Family-Friendly Features: *pirate battle every 90 minutes at entrance to hotel, Mutiny Bay amusement center with virtual reality games and arcade games, pool complex, Mystere by Cirque du Soleil show*

Part of the Mirage family, Treasure Island has several family-friendly attractions that make children feel comfortable at this hotel. You can't miss the pirate battle held every 90 minutes just outside the hotel, complete with the sinking of a ship. Inside, the atmosphere is more elegant than you might expect with several fine dining restaurants and a spa. The hotel does welcome families, however, and they'll find an extensive pool complex , Mystere by Cirque du Soleil, and Mutiny Bay, the adventure amusement center featuring arcade, virtual reality and interactive games.

This hotel recently underwent a $65 million renovation of its 2900 guest rooms. Rooms now include wooden armoires with entertainment centers, marble baths and showers, and excellent views of the Strip, Buccaneer Bay Village, the mountains, or the pool.

BUILD IT AND THEY WILL COME

Las Vegas is booming. In 1999, the city hosted 33.8 million visitors. That's up 10.5% from the figures in 1998! The city's hotel room inventory also grew 10%, rising to over 120,000 rooms. Even with all those rooms, though, finding one can be tough. The average occupancy rate was 88 percent. How does that compare to other cities around the US? The average hotel occupancy rate in the US is 65 percent.

OTHER RECOMMENDED CASINO HOTELS ON THE STRIP

ALADDIN

3667 Las Vegas Boulevard South, Tel. 702/736-0111 or 800/634-3424, Fax 702/734-3583, www.aladdincasino.com.

Rates: *$$-$$$*
Amenities: *two casinos, health spa, shopping*
Family-friendly features: *pool*

At press time, this new theme casino-hotel had not yet opened so we haven't had the chance to view its facilities. It sounds like this will be another excellent addition to the Strip, however, taking on an Aladdin theme.

BALLY'S CASINO RESORT

3645 Las Vegas Boulevard South, Tel. 702/739-4111 or 800/634-3434, Fax 702/739-4405, www.ballyslv.com.

Rates: *$$-$$$*
Amenities: *two showrooms, spa, shopping mall, five restaurants, major special events center, retail area*
Family-friendly features: *Olympic sized pool, monorail to MGM Grand*

The first time we stayed at Bally's we encountered a full house in our room category and we were bumped up to the next category. What we encountered was Vegas classic: a round bed with gold spread, all on a raised platform. Ever since then, we've loved this casino hotel, but is it good for families? We think it's a pretty good choice for several reasons: location, location, location. You'll find most of the glitzy theme casino hotels within walking distance.

BARBARY COAST

3595 Las Vegas Boulevard South, Tel. 702/737-7111 or 888/227-2279, 702/737-6304, www.barbarycoastcasino.com.

Rates: *$-$$*
Amenities: *casino, three restaurants*
Family-friendly features: *bowling*

This 196-room hotel features a Victorian decor, from oak paneling down to stained glass. The guest rooms have a more modern feel, thanks to textured wallpaper, glass accents, and etched mirrors.

BELLAGIO – THE RESORT

3600 Las Vegas Boulevard South, Tel. 702/693-7444, 888/987-3456, www.bellagiolasvegas.com.

Rates: *$$$*
Amenities: *casino, 10 restaurants, golf, botanical gardens, spa, salon*
Family-friendly features: *Bellagio fountains, "O" show by Cirque du Soleil*

The Bellagio is an adults' hotel and they have made a policy that we appreciate: children under age 18 are only permitted if they are guests of the hotel. Think it's odd that we, the authors of a family travel guide, approve of such a policy? Not at all. This hotel recognizes its market – that of adults on vacation – and targets that market.

That's not to say you can't stay here with your family; you can. And as non-guests, you can even bring your kids in, if the circumstances are right. (Non-guest children of at least five years old are permitted on property for dining at Aqua, Circo, Jasmine, Le

Cirque, Picasso, Shintaro or Prime restaurants; to attend a wedding; to attend a convention function; to attend a performance of "O"; to visit the Gallery of Fine Art.)

VEGAS ON FILM

Las Vegas has starred in plenty of movies, but it's not easy to find some suitable for the whole family. (Hey, do you really want your kids to watch Vegas Vacation or Showgirls before you hit the Strip?) Here are a few G-rated selections that are fun for everyone, though:

Las Vegas Kidz Adventure Video
This videotape is designed for kids ages 5-14 and covers, in half an hour, the highlights of the city. The videotape is packaged with a set of crayons so children can color the cover. The video includes sights such as Adventuredome, Hoover Dam, Wet 'n Wild, MGM Theme Park, Valley of Fire, and more.

Las Vegas Hillbillys (1966)
This Jayne Mansfield movie, rated G, follows two country singers as they come to the glittery city.

Viva Las Vegas (1963)
Elvis plays a racecar driver in town for the big race in this fun movie that costars Ann-Margret.

CAESARS PALACE
3570 Las Vegas Boulevard South, Tel. 702/731-7110, Fax 702/731-7172, www.caesars.com.

Rates: *$$-$$$*
Amenities: *many rooms with Roman tubs or whirlpool baths, business center, health spa*

Family-friendly features: *Fountain Show at Forum Shops, motion rides*

This hotel also has a moving sidewalk to sweep you and your family inside to the world of Caesar's Rome. On the way in, you'll move past a hologram diorama of ancient Rome. Families will also enjoy the costumed "Romans." There is still a video arcade for kids. One word of advice about Caesars: get a map as soon as you enter. This is a sprawling hotel, and you can easily lose your way.

DESERT INN
3201 Las Vegas Boulevard North, Tel. 800/634-6909, www.desertinn.com.

Rates: *$$$*
Amenities: *715 rooms, 200 acres on the Strip, 18-hole golf course, European spa, gourmet dining, casino, two showrooms*
Family-friendly features: *pool*

The Desert Inn just celebrated its 50th year on the Strip with a $200 million renovation. It boasts the only golf course located on the Strip and a full range of other services. The 715-room hotel includes luxury features such as modem lines, hair dryer, and express checkout via TV remote control.

FLAMINGO HILTON
3555 Las Vegas Boulevard South, Tel. 702/733-3111 or 800/732-2111, Fax 702/733-3353, www.lv-flamingo.com.

Rates: *$-$$$*
Amenities: *casino, health club, exercise room*
Family-friendly features: *baby-sitting services, 15 acre water playground, flamingo habitat, "The Voice of Magic with Darren Romeo" show*

TOTS & TOPLESS WOMEN

You can stay out of the topless shows but it's tough to completely avoid Las Vegas's sex industry. Flyers are distributed on the street to promote strip clubs with images of scantily clad (make that un-clad) women. With kids by your side, you won't be offered flyers but a few steps away be prepared to see discarded flyers littering the ground. Just be prepared.

This hotel was long one of the best known in Las Vegas, the place that Bugsy Siegal built. Today it's part of the Hilton chain but, to sound cool, just call it the Flamingo. It has been renovated and now has 3,642 rooms.

Even if you're not staying here, don't miss the flamingo habitat, filled with Chilean flamingos as well as African penguins, swans, ducks, turtles, and more.

FOUR SEASONS HOTEL LAS VEGAS
3960 Las Vegas Boulevard South, Tel. 702/632-5000 or 877/632-5000, www.fourseasons.com.

Rates: *$$$*
Amenities: *health club, twice daily housekeeping, in-room coffee service, five restaurants, room service*
Family-friendly features: *No gaming, 8000-square-foot pool*

The Four Seasons is a breath of fresh air along the Strip; there is no gaming at this exclusive, luxurious property and its atmosphere is calmer and quieter. The more serene atmosphere begins at the entrance which, unlike most other Strip properties, is set back off the bustling street by a private drive. Once inside, you'll be met by muted Mediterranean colors, marble floors, and simple statuary. It's not a kids' resort, but its quieter feel is a good retreat for families.

The location of the resort is also a Vegas first: the hotel is actually located in Mandalay Bay, floors 35 to 39. The guest rooms are accessed only by private elevators (the lobby is located in a two-story greathouse at the entrance). Suites are especially popular with families and can be configured to include three bedrooms. (OK, you need to be an heir of Howard Hughes or have hit the jackpot to afford one of these suites, but we're just giving you the options.)

HARRAH'S

3475 Las Vegas Boulevard South, Tel. 702/369-5000 or 800/427-7247, Fax 702/369-5008, www. harrahs.lv.com.

Rates: *$-$$$*
Amenities: *casino, six restaurants, deli, health club, shopping, spa, salon*
Family-friendly features: *Pool, Carnaval Court, video arcade, magic show*

This 2700-room hotel is definitely aimed at adults, but kids will enjoy Carnaval Court, the outdoor piazza with the feel of a street fair.

IMPERIAL PALACE

3535 Las Vegas Boulevard South, Tel. 702/731-3311 or 800/634-6441, Fax 702/735-8578, www.imperialpalace.com.

Rates: *$-$$*
Amenities: *casino, spa, wedding chapel*

Family-friendly features: *heated Olympic-size pool, Imperial Palace Auto Collection, Legends in Concert show, Hawaiian Hot Luau, "Backstage Live" radio show*

This centrally-located casino hotel is home to several attractions that might be of interest to some members of the family. Along with the **Imperial Palace Auto Collection**, the hotel hosts **"Legends in Concert,"** a look at some of music's most famous faces...well, at least impersonators of those famous faces. You never know who might drop in for the Backstage Live show, a free radio show that recently featured Rich Little.

During peak months (April through October), the hotel's pool area hosts **Hawaiian Hot Luau**, a nightly dinner and show, complete with firedancers and a tropical feel.

MANDALAY BAY
3950 Las Vegas Boulevard South, Tel. 702/632-7777 or 877/632-7000, Fax 702/632-7919, www.mandalaybay.com.

Rates: *$$-$$$*
Amenities: *casino, two phone lines, 27" television, 12 restaurants*
Family-Friendly Features: *11-acre tropical lagoon*

Mandalay Bay's top family feature is its 11-acre tropical lagoon. It's surf and sand on the Strip here, complete with a Lazy River Ride and three pools. Along the water's edge, you'll find cabanas and lounges to hide from the desert sun.

Rooms at Mandalay Bay are all generously sized, averaging about 500 square feet. Each includes a master bath with stone floors and counters, a separate tub and shower, blow dryer, make-up mirror, his and hers lighted closets, two phone lines, 27-inch television, and more.

MIRAGE

3400 Las Vegas Boulevard South, Tel. 702/791-7.. 6667, Fax 702/791-7446, www.themirage.com.

Rates: *$$$*
Amenities: *casino, spa, nine specialty restaurants, salon*

Family-friendly Features: *swimming pool, white tiger habitat, dolphin habitat, saltwater aquarium, tropical rainforest, volcano*

The first of Las Vegas's theme hotels, The Mirage is still one of our favorites, tastefully done and magically enchanting. The hotel includes 3044 guest rooms but it's best known for its amenities and stylish attractions. Out front stands the volcano, a pyrotechnic attraction that blows throughout the evening. Inside, the enchanting feel of the South Seas starts with a larger than life aquarium at check-in, and continues with tropical rainforest, streams, birds, waterfalls, and more.

The hotel has long been the home of Siegfried and Roy, the city's best-known magic act. The two feature white tigers in their act, and, when not performing, the tigers can be seen at the Tiger Habitat. The hotel is also home to the Dolphin Habitat and the Secret Garden.

Guest rooms here are tastefully done in shades of beige and peach, with one king or two queen beds.

MONTE CARLO

3770 Las Vegas Boulevard South, Tel. 702/730-7777 or 800/311-8999, Fax 702/730-7200, www.monte-carlo.com.

Rates: *$-$$$*
Amenities: *24-hour room service, casino, shopping areas, seven restaurants*

Family-Friendly Features: *large pool area, Lance Burton magic show*

This 3002-room hotel is pure elegance, sporting a turn-of-the century decor. Even the standard rooms are elegant, with Italian marble touches and cherry furniture (a surprise when you look at the $60 mid-week prices!) The hotel has a shopping pavilion (Brats has designer clothes for kids) and the Lance Burton magic show from Thursday-Sunday.

NEW YORK-NEW YORK HOTEL AND CASINO

3790 Las Vegas Boulevard, Tel. 702/740-6969 or 800/693-6763, Fax 702/891-5285, www.nynyhotelcasino.com.

Rates: *$$-$$$*
Amenities: *casino, restaurant, fitness center*
Family-Friendly Features: *Manhattan Express roller coaster, arcade, pool*

Ready for the Big Apple? It's all here at this theme resort that starts with a recreation of the Manhattan skyline (OK, there's a roller coaster buzzing around it, but still, it's the skyline complete with 12 "skyscrapers"). The hotel has over 2000 guest rooms and carries out its theme with everything from a casino with a theme of Central Park to a 300-foot-long replica of the Brooklyn Bridge to a 150-foot replica of the Statue of Liberty.

This 2,034-room hotel doesn't cater to children as much as the MGM Grand (there's no supervised children's program here) but kids will find the Coney Island Emporium, an arcade with everything from laser tag to virtual reality games. It's all set with the feel of Coney Island. Check out the Coney Island Emporium entry in the "What Are We Doing Next?" chapter for more on this attraction.

PARIS LAS VEGAS

3655 Las Vegas Boulevard South, Tel. 702/946-7000 or 877/796-2096, www.paris-lv.com.

Rates: *$-$$$*

Amenities: *marble bathrooms, pay-per-view movies, on-command video, cable television, two-line phones, voice mail, hair dryer, data-port, four concierge floors, 24-hour room service, tour and travel desk, connected to Bally's/MGM monorail system, complimentary valet parking, European health spa*

Family-friendly features: *roof-top swimming pool, Eiffel Tower Experience with ride in glass elevator to top of the Eiffel Tower replica*

This 2,916-room hotel is one of the Strip's newest, bringing the atmosphere of Paris here in a slick $760 million package. The hotel is filled with the feel of France, from its boutiques to its restaurants, although the atmosphere here is definitely for adults and not kids. Children will enjoy the symbol of Paris, however, with a ride up the 50-story (half size) replica of the Eiffel Tower. (There's a gourmet restaurant in the tower, but save this for another trip when the kids are at their grandparents' house.) Other landmark replicas here include Hotel de Ville and façades of the Paris Opera House and The Louvre.

In keeping with its name, this hotel has European fixtures and plenty of French fabrics.

RIVIERA

2901 Las Vegas Boulevard South, Tel. 702/734-5110 or 800/634-6753, Fax 702/794-9451, www.theriviera.com.

Rates: *$$*

Amenities: *Three restaurants and a buffet, a 24-hour coffee shop, food court, health club, over 45 shops, two tennis courts, casino*

Family-friendly Features: *many rooms with poolside patios, pool, arcade*

For over 40 years, this 2100-room hotel has been a popular stop along the Strip. Recently all its guest rooms underwent renovation and the hotel now provides a fresher face. This hotel is really one for adults, though (you might think otherwise since it's the home of the show Splash which, in spite of its name, is topless).

The hotel does have some features that make it attractive to families, though. You'll find the Mardi Gras Food Court here for inexpensive meals at eateries like Burger King, Panda Express, Pizza Hut, and others. Kady's Coffee Shop is open 24 hours for breakfast, lunch or dinner. There are also numerous shops here with wares that range from magic to sports and celebrity memorabilia.

SAHARA HOTEL AND CASINO
2535 Las Vegas Boulevard South, Tel. 702/737-2111 or 800/634-6666, Fax 702/791-2027, www.pcap.com/sahara.htm.

Rates: *$-$$*
Amenities: *casino*
Family-Friendly **Features**: *two swimming pools, shopping, Sahara Speedworld, Speed – The Ride rollercoaster*

This 1709-room hotel is currently undergoing a major renovation which promises to give it a North African theme. Although the hotel is aimed at adults, it does offer family-friendly features like its popular Sahara Speedworld, with virtual reality games. The hotel also has a large shopping promenade.

STARDUST

3000 Las Vegas Boulevard South, Tel. 702/732-6111 or 800/824-6033, Fax 702/732-6257, www.stardustlv.com

Rates: *$-$$$*
Amenities: *casino, five restaurants*
Family-Friendly **Features**: *two swimming pools, video arcade*

This long-running hotel is scheduled for a major facelift soon, one that will give the property a Moroccan theme. Look for major changes here soon. The hotel includes a video arcade but is best known as the showplace of "Mr. Las Vegas," Wayne Newton.

STRATOSPHERE

2000 Las Vegas Boulevard South, Tel. 702/380-7777 or 800/998-6937, Fax 702/383-5334, www.stratlv.com.

Rates: *$-$$*
Amenities: *casino, fine dining, showroom, retail shopping*
Family-Friendly **Features**: *Pepsi Cola Observation decks, Big Shot, High Roller, video arcade, pool*

You can't miss the Stratosphere, just look for the tallest building in the state of Nevada (actually TWICE the height of any other building in the state). In fact, this soaring piece of steel is the tallest building west of the Mississippi River.

It may be best known for its tower, but this is also a hotel with 1500 rooms. All rooms have in-room safes and hair dryers, with either one king or, for families, two queen-sized beds. Plans are underway for the completion of a new tower with over 1000 guest rooms, a 67,000-square-foot swimming pool, and two spas.

n't interested in hotel rooms, they're interested in tratosphere, that fun lies above your head. You can si Cola Observation Deck for a 360-degree view of the city at a height of 857 feet above the ground or, for a real thrill, go up a level to the outdoor observation deck. This outdoor deck is also a good place to watch visitors braving the Big Shot and High Roller, two thrill rides we won't brave but we'll tell you about in the "What Are We Doing Next?" chapter.

TROPICANA RESORT AND CASINO

3801 Las Vegas Boulevard South, Tel. 702/739-2222 or 800/634-4000, Fax 702/739-2469, www.tropicanalv.com.

Rates: *$-$$*
Amenities: *casino, health club, five restaurants*
Family-Friendly Features: *water park, wildlife walk, world's largest indoor/outdoor swimming pool*

With its South Pacific theme, the Tropicana has long been one of our favorites. Now with additional family features (plus a great location in easy walking distance of the MGM Grand, Excalibur, Luxor and New York New York), this is a good destination for families.

Rooms here include the Garden Rooms, located in three story buildings around the park and garden area (a good choice for families). The Island Tower rooms, the back tower but near the pool area, have two queen beds or one king with a pullout sofa. Paradise Tower rooms are the premium rooms (they've recently been remodeled); each of these has one king or two queens (good for families) and added amenities including a refrigerator.

Today this hotel casino is home to a five-acre water park filled with lagoons and waterfalls. It's so huge the Tropicana calls this the world's largest indoor/outdoor swimming pool. The hotel is also home to the Wildlife Walk, with birds and wildlife in a tropical setting.

THE VENETIAN

3355 Las Vegas Boulevard South, Tel. 702/733-5000, www.venetian.com.

Rates: *$$-$$$*
Amenities: *casino, 24-hour complimentary valet parking, 24-hour room service, travel bureau*
Family-Friendly **Features**: *gondola rides, Madame Tussaud's, Theatres of Sensation 3-D Motion Rides*

According to Guinness Book of World Records, The Venetian has the largest hotel rooms in the world. The 3036 standard guest rooms have 700 square feet of living space that includes everything from a marble foyer to an Italian marble bath. Room amenities include two 27-inch TVs, a mini bar, fax machine, three phones, a sofa that opens to a queen size bed, and more.

This hotel is really aimed at adults and has a quiet, romantic atmosphere. Families will feel comfortable here, though, and will enjoy the attractions like the gondola rides, the wax museum, and the Theatres of Sensation. The kids will also like the Venetian's pool deck. There are five swimming pools on property so you'll find plenty of chances to cool off on a hot summer's day.

VACATION VILLAGE

6711 Las Vegas Boulevard South, Tel. 702/897-1700 or 800/658-5000, Fax 702/361-6726, www.vacationvillagevegas.com.

Rates: *$*
Amenities: *casino, Denny's Restaurant, buffet, other restaurants, complimentary airport shuttle*

Family-Friendly **Features**: *two outdoor pools, arcade*

During low season, prices start at $30 a room midweek, so this property is a bargain. The 317-room hotel has a Southwestern decor and has an arcade for kids as well as two pools.

WESTWARD HO HOTEL AND CASINO
2900 Las Vegas Boulevard South, Tel. 702/731-2900 or 800/634-6803, Fax 702/735-5211, www.westwardho.com.

Rates: *$*
Amenities: *casino, 24-hour restaurant*
Family-Friendly **Features**: *seven pools*

This 777-room hotel is located on the north end of the Strip, next to the Circus Circus.

CASINO RULES

Casino rules are strict and straightforward: no one under 21 is allowed in the gaming areas. This doesn't just mean that kids can't gamble, but you cannot stop and drop that quarter in the slot machine on your stroll with Junior through the casino. Keep walking!

HOTELS OFF THE STRIP
ALEXIS PARK RESORT AND SPA
375 East Harmon, Tel. 702/796-3300 or 800/582-2228, Fax 702/796-4334, www.alexispark.com.

Rates: *$$-$$$*
Amenities: *restaurant, lobby bar, 24-hour golf driving range adjacent to hotel, fitness center and spa*

Family-Friendly **Features**: *non-gaming hotel, three pools, tennis*

This sophisticated resort offers a quiet respite from the hustle and bustle of the Strip. With 500 guest suites, families will appreciate the Standard Suite. At 450-600 square feet, the rooms include a queen or two double beds. Larger suites include two-story suites.

BEST WESTERN MARDI GRAS INN

3500 Paradise Road, Tel. 702/731-2020 or 800/634-6501, Fax 702/731-4005, www.mardigrasinn.com.

Rates: *$-$$*

Amenities: *casino, salon, restaurants, mini-suites, free shuttle to airport and Strip*

Family-friendly facilities: *pool, complimentary Continental breakfast, picnic area*

Located a block from the convention center, this hotel is a popular choice with convention delegates and their families, but it also has many attractive features for families on pure vacation as well. The hotel has 314 mini-suites, each with a separate living area, a wet bar and refrigerator, color TV with in-room movies, and more.

COURTYARD BY MARRIOTT, CONVENTION CENTER

3275 Paradise Rd, Tel. 702/791-3600 or 800/321-2211, Fax 702/796-7981, www.courtyard.com/LASCH/

Rates: *$$*

Amenities: *four restaurants, room service, exercise room*

Family-friendly facilities: *pool, cribs available*

This 149-room motel was designed for the business traveler, but families find several good features including the complimentary airport shuttle and pool.

CROWNE PLAZA HOLIDAY INN

4255 S. Paradise Road, Tel. 702/369-4400 or 800/465-4329, Fax 702/369-3770, www.crowneplaza.com.

Rates: *$$$*
Amenities: *gym, hot tub*
Family-friendly facilities: *pool*

This hotel is convenient to the Convention Center, the airport, and is only two blocks from the Strip. Much of the hotel's clientele are business travelers and conventioneers.

EMBASSY SUITES - AIRPORT

4315 Swenson, Tel. 702/795-2800 or 800/EMBASSY, www.embassy-suites.com.

Rates: *$$*
Amenities: *complimentary airport shuttle*
Family-friendly facilities: *cribs available, pool*

Located adjacent to the Hard Rock Hotel and Casino, this hotel also is just a short drive from the Strip (about a mile).

EMBASSY SUITES CONVENTION CENTER

3600 Paradise Road, Tel. 702/893-8000 or 800/EMBASSY, www.embassy-suites.com.

Rates: *$$*
Amenities: *complimentary airport shuttle, exercise room*
Family-friendly facilities: *heated indoor pool*

This new hotel is about three blocks from the Convention Center so it's a favorite with meeting attendees and their families. The hotel has 286 suites and all guests enjoy a complimentary breakfast (a full cooked-to-order deal, not a bowl of cereal and a cold roll). During the evening, guests also enjoy a reception with snacks and beverages.

EMERALD SPRINGS HOLIDAY INN

325 East Flamingo Rd, Tel. 702/732-9100 or 800/732-7889, Fax 702/731-9784, www.holidayinnlasvegas.com.

Rates: *$$*
Amenities: *spa, concierge service, restaurant, complimentary limo service to airport*
Family-friendly facilities: *no gaming, pool, Nintendo games available for checkout*

This hotel has 150 guest rooms and suites and is located four blocks form the Strip. Kids will appreciate the hotel's collection of Nintendo games available for room checkout.

GOLD COAST

4000 West Flamingo Road, Tel. 702/367-7111 or 800/331-5334, Fax 702/367-8419, www.goldcoastcasino.com.

Rates: *$*
Amenities: *casino, five restaurants, bingo parlor, dance hall*
Family-friendly facilities: *two movie theaters, free child care center, swimming pool*

Decorated in Spanish style, this casino hotel is located a mile west of the Strip. Offering 750 guest rooms, the Gold Coast isn't a luxury property but offers a lot of family diversions for the price.

HARD ROCK HOTEL

4455 Paradise Road, Tel. 702/693-5000 or 800/413-1635, Fax 702/693-5010, www.hardrockhotel.com .

Rates: *$-$$$*
Amenities: *casino, three restaurants, health club*
Family-friendly facilities: *large pool area, Hard Rock Cafe*

Why didn't we pick the Hard Rock Hotel as one of the best kid-friendly hotels? Because it's not. You might think the Hard Rock would be a great place to take kids but, take our word for it, this hotel is not aimed at children. It's not aimed at their parents. It's aimed at twenty-something travelers who are hipper than you ever were and with more energy than you'll ever have again. Take the kids here and you'll feel like ugly ducklings in a pond of swans; take your teenagers here and you'll feel like dinosaurs and just reinforce their notions that you are definitely too old to have any fun with.

Look elsewhere for a family getaway. With a theater called The Joint and a restaurant called the Pink Taco, the family just ain't going to fit in here.

HAWTHORN SUITES

5051 Duke Ellington Way, Tel. 702/739-7000 or 800/527-1133, Fax 702/739-9350, www.hawthorn.com.

Rates: *$-$$*
Amenities: *exercise room, sports club, hot tubs, complimentary evening social hour*
Family-friendly facilities: *in-room movies, video games, pool, no gaming, complimentary buffet breakfast*

Just a short hop off the Strip, this hotel has suites that are ideal for families including full kitchens, complimentary coffee, two TVs, and even complimentary buffet breakfast.

HOTEL SAN REMO

115 E. Tropicana Avenue, Tel. 702/739-9000 or 800/522-7366, Fax 702/736-1120, www.sanremolasvegas.com.

Rates: *$-$$$*
Amenities: *casino, five restaurants, room service*
Family-friendly facilities: *pool*

This 711-room hotel has a more elegant decor that you might expect off the Strip, with several Jacuzzi suites.

KEY LARGO CASINO AT QUALITY INN

377 East Flamingo Road, Tel. 702/733-7777 or 800/634-6617, Fax 702/369-6911, www.keylargocasino.com,

Rates: *$-$$*
Amenities: *casino, poolside bar, spa, complimentary airport shuttle*
Family-friendly facilities: *heated outdoor pool*

This 320-room hotel features mini-suites, each with refrigerators, wet bars, in-room coffee, and cable TV with in-room movies.

LA QUINTA

3970 Paradise Road, Tel. 702/796-9000 or 800/531-5900, Fax 702/796-3537, www.laquinta.com.

Rates: *$*
Amenities: *hot tub, modem lines in rooms, free shuttle*
Family-friendly facilities: *pool, kids under 18 stay free, family units/suites, free continental breakfast*

This 251-room hotel is casino-free and an easy choice for families, thanks to its "kids under 18 stay free" policy as well as its free continental breakfast (where you'll find cereal for those young travelers), and family units. These 51 one- and two-bedroom units include microwaves. The hotel also offers a free airport shuttle.

LAS VEGAS HILTON

3000 Paradise Road, Tel. 702/732-5111 or 800/732-7117, Fax 702/794-3611, www.lv-hilton.com.

Rates: $$-$$$
Amenities: *casino, health club, spa, eight restaurants*
Family-friendly facilities: *Star Trek: The Experience, pool*

The Hilton boasts over 3000 guest rooms and suites, all with cable TV, multiple phones, and connecting rooms – a nice feature for families with teens who want their own space. The Star Trek Experience, an interactive attraction, is a sure winner with kids.

LAS VEGAS MARRIOTT SUITES

325 Convention Center Drive, Tel. 702/650-2000 or 800/244-3364, Fax 702/650-9466, www.marriotthotels.com/LASST.

Rates: $$$
Amenities: *restaurant, data ports on phones, in-room movies, newspaper on weekdays, in-room coffee*
Family-friendly facilities: *cribs available*

The 278 suites at this property, which is located a block west of the Las Vegas Convention Center, makes it nice for families looking for a little bit of elbow room. All the rooms include a sitting area, a mini refrigerator, a coffee maker, and a separate bedroom.

ORLEANS

4500 W. Tropicana, Tel. 702/365-7111 or 800/ORLEANS, Fax 702/365-7535, www.orleanscasino.com.

Rates: *$*

Amenities: *casino, complimentary shuttle to Barbary Coast and Gold Coast, seven restaurants, fitness center*

Family-friendly facilities: *movie theaters, supervised children's care program, bowling center, pool complex, arcade*

Located a mile west of the Strip, this hotel is styled with all the fun of Mardi Gras. The 810 guest rooms are roomy but the real attraction here are the hotel's numerous assets. Along with seven restaurants (everything from Cajun to fast food), the hotel includes a 70-lane bowling center, a 12-screen movie complex, an arcade with video as well as interactive games, a large pool complex and more. Parents interested in a little time to gamble will appreciate the supervised children's program (see "Who's Going to Take Care of Me?").

PALACE STATION HOTEL

2411 W. Sahara Avenue, Tel. 702/367-2411 or 800/634-3101, Fax 702/221-6510, www.palacestation.com.

Rates: *$-$$$*

Amenities: *casino, shuttle service, gift shop, tour and show ticket desk, room service, five restaurants*

Family-friendly facilities: *video arcade, two pools*

This 1028-room casino hotel is a favorite with locals.

RESIDENCE INN BY MARRIOTT

3225 Paradise Road, Tel. 702/796-9300 or 800/331-3131, Fax 702/796-6571, www.residenceinn.com/LASVN.

Rates: *$$*
Amenities:*full kitchen with refrigerator in all rooms, in-room movies*
Family-friendly facilities: *cribs available*

Like other Residence Inns, this property is designed to make travelers feel right at home. The 192 studio or penthouse rooms here have the feel of a home away from home, complete with a full kitchen. The hotel also offers complimentary breakfast as well as a light dinner on weekdays. An airport shuttle service is also available.

RIO SUITES HOTEL AND CASINO

3700 W. Flamingo Road, Tel. 702/252-7777 or 800/752-9746, Fax 702/253-6090, www.playrio.com.

Rates: *$$*
Amenities: *casino, fitness center, numerous restaurants*
Family-friendly facilities: *Masquerade Village Show in the Sky, three pools, Titanic exhibit, Footloose show*

The Rio is especially known for its large guest rooms: each 600 square feet with a refrigerator, coffee maker, iron and ironing board, and blow dryer.

ST. TROPEZ

455 East Harmon, Tel. 702/369-5400 or 800/666-5400, Fax 702/369-1150, www.sttropezlasvegas.com.

Rates: *$$-$$$*

Amenities: *exercise gym, spa, complimentary Continental breakfast, complimentary airport shuttle*
Family-friendly facilities: *no gaming, pool, TV/VCR in all rooms*

This all-suite hotel is a good choice for families in search of a little elbow room. It's also a non-gaming property, a good choice for families looking to get away from the casino flurry.

BOULDER STRIP HOTELS
BOULDER STATION
4111 Boulder Highway, Tel. 702/432-7777 or 800/683-7777, Fax 702/432-7730.

Rates: *$-$$*
Amenities: *casino, live entertainment, 24-hour coffee shop, six restaurants*
Family-friendly facilities: *pool*

This 300-room hotel is a favorite gaming spot for local residents and well-known for its friendly staff.

NEVADA PALACE
5255 Boulder Highway, Tel. 702/458-8810 or 800/634-6283, Fax 702/458-3361, www.pcap.com/nvpalace.htm.

Rates: *$-$$*
Amenities: *casino, RV park, 24-hour restaurant*
Family-friendly facilities: *pool*

Nevada Palace is located about 15 minutes from the city out on the Boulder Highway. The 220-room hotel's draw is its low rates, along with its casino. The hotel offers a trucker's special, so don't expect to see this one filled with families.

SAM'S TOWN

5111 Boulder Highway, Tel. 702/456-7777 or 800/634-6371, Fax 702/454-8014, www.samstownlv.com.

Rates: *$*
Amenities: *casino, RV park, 10 restaurants, sports bar, dance hall*
Family-friendly facilities: *food court, indoor park, bowling, Sunset Stampede at Mystic Park Falls*

This Old West themed hotel has 650 rooms, each continuing the Western motif.

SHOWBOAT

2800 East Fremont Street, Tel. 702/385-9123 or 800/826-2800, Fax 702/383-9238, www.showboat-lv.com.

Rates: *$-$$*
Amenities: *casino*
Family-friendly facilities: *North America's largest bowling center, outdoor pool*

Showboat was the first casino hotel we ever stayed at in Las Vegas, one we stumbled on completely by accident. To tell the truth, the whole time we were there, we were wondering why we weren't on The Strip, where all the fun was. It's a nice enough hotel, but, if you're not a die-hard bowler, the fun here is limited. The hotel's theme is that of a Mississippi riverboat. Perhaps it's that theme or maybe it's the bowling, but this hotel seems to attract a much older crowd than the Strip properties.

DOWNTOWN HOTELS

BINION'S HORSESHOE

128 East Fremont, Tel. 702/382-1600 or 800/237-6537, Fax 702/382-5750.

Rates: *$*
Amenities: *24-hour restaurant*
Family-friendly facilities: *rooftop pool*

This hotel is a favorite with serious gamblers thanks to its annual tournaments. This is an old-fashioned Vegas hotel, with the emphasis on gaming. High rollers are far more common here than high chairs.

CALIFORNIA HOTEL

12 Ogden Avenue, Tel. 702/385-1222 or 800/634-6255, Fax 702/388-2660, www.thecal.com.

Rates: *$-$$*
Amenities: *casino, RV park, four restaurants*
Family-friendly facilities: *children under 12 stay free in parents' room, video arcade, pool, candy shop*

This 800-room hotel prides itself on its "Aloha Spirit." Let's see...it's called the California, it's located in Nevada, but it has Aloha Spirit!

FITZGERALD'S CASINO HOLIDAY INN

301 East Fremont Street, Tel. 702/388-2400 or 800/274-5825, Fax 702/388-2181, www.vegas.fitzgeralds.com.

Rates: *$-$$*
Amenities: *casino, five restaurants*
Family-friendly facilities: *McDonald's*

This 650-room tower hotel is a downtown fixture. Each room has a safe, 25 inch TV, and modem ports.

FOUR QUEENS

202 East Fremont Street, Tel. 702/385-4011 or 800/634-6045, Fax 702/387-5122, www.fourqueens.com.

Rates: *$*
Amenities: *casino, three restaurants*
Family-friendly facilities: *Burger King*

This 700-room high rise hotel features Jacuzzis in some suites.

GOLD SPIKE

400 East Ogden Avenue, Tel. 702/384-8444 or 800/634-6703, Fax 702/384-8768, www.goldspikehotelcasino.com.

Rates: *$*
Amenities: *casino, lounge*
Family-friendly facilities: *childcare facility, free breakfast daily*

With 109 rooms, the Gold Spike is one of the more kid-friendly hotels in the downtown area thanks to its childcare facility.

GOLDEN GATE HOTEL AND CASINO

111 South Main Street, Tel. 702/382-3510 or 800/426-1906, Fax 702/382-5349.

Rates: *$*
Amenities: *casino, restaurant*
Family-friendly facilities: *near Fremont Street Experience*

The Golden Gate is one of the oldest hotels in the city and has a more intimate atmosphere than other properties thanks to its

HELP YOUR CHILD BRING HOME VACATION MEMORIES

Every vacationer wants to return home with memories of the experience that will help him relive the trip time after time. Adults rely on cameras to capture these memories, but children all too often fall prey to overpriced souvenirs as a poor substitute.

There is a way to help your child bring back vacation memories – without breaking your trip budget. No matter where you travel, free (or low cost) souvenirs are yours for the asking. Your children can collect everything ranging from postcards to matchbooks and placemats. They are available in restaurants, campgrounds, motels, tourist attractions, and service stations, potentially every place your family might stop. By showing your child the fun of searching for (not just buying) souvenirs, you can involve him in the excitement of seeking out free souvenirs and keep him away from the trinket stands which plague so many tourist attractions.

Your first step begins before the vacation at your neighborhood five-and-dime. Buy each child an inexpensive photo album ($1-2) with adhesive pages. These pages allow small fingers to stick memorabilia in the book, and they will survive several rearrangements before you have to resort to glue.

Keep an eye out for these souvenirs:

Restaurants: You'll find special children's placemats in many family restaurants, often with pictures or a map of local attractions. Free children's menus, containing a game or a puzzle, are available in many restaurants. And don't overlook tiny sugar packets with the restaurant's name or picture on it. These can act as miniature postcards, ready to assume a place in your child's scrapbook.

Postcards: For about a quarter each, you can carry home a professional photo of almost any attraction in the world. These are a great bargain, and a much better buy than the slides sold at many places, which have often faded under fluorescent lights. And if you've heard your child complain "I never get any mail," encourage them to send a postcard to themselves! They'll act as miniature vacation diaries when they return home, and give returning vacationers a little something to look forward to as well.

Matchbooks: Many restaurants and hotels give away free matchbooks. Minus the matches, of course, these make good additions to the scrapbook. Also, your young travelers may want to start a matchbook collection in a jar once they return home.

small size – just 106 guest rooms. With almost a B&B feel, this hotel is just steps from the Fremont Street Experience (see the "What Are We Doing Next?" chapter for more).

GOLDEN NUGGET

129 East Fremont Street, Tel. 702/385-7111 or 800/634-3454, Fax 702/386-8362, www.goldennugget.com.

Rates: *$-$$*
Amenities: *casino, five restaurants, spa, outdoor Jacuzzi*
Family-friendly facilities: *Olympic sized heated pool*

This 1805-room casino hotel is a AAA Four Diamond property and known for its elegance, from its crystal chandeliers to its fine marble. The hotel has several elegant features as well such as a spa

JACKIE GAUGHAN'S PLAZA

1 Main Street, Tel. 702/386-2110 or 800/634-6575, Fax 702/382-8281, www.plazahotelcasino.com.

Rates: *$*
Amenities: *casino, tennis, 24-hour coffee shop, restaurant*
Family-friendly facilities: *pool, video arcade, ice cream parlor*

This 1037-room hotel is a downtown fixture. Although it's best known for its casino, it does have some family friendly features as well as good prices.

LADY LUCK CASINO AND HOTEL

206 N. 3rd Street, Tel. 702/477-3000 or 800/921-1957, Fax 702/477-3002, www.ladyluck.com.

Rates: *$*
Amenities: *casino, four restaurants*

Family-friendly facilities: *pool*

This 791-room hotel has rooms with refrigerators, a plus for families, and very family-friendly prices, with rooms starting at $39 per night.

MAIN STREET STATION

200 N. Main Street, Tel. 702/387-1896 or 800/465-0711, Fax 702/386-4421, www.mainstreetcasino.com.

Rates: *$-$$*
Amenities: *casino, micro-brewery, gourmet dining, 24-hour cafe*
Family-friendly facilities: *good location*

This 406-room hotel has a Victorian era theme and recently underwent an upgrade. You'll see Victorian touches everywhere, from sconces to rich paneling. The rooms continue the decorating scheme with gold framed mirrors, white window shutters, and rich woods.

MONEY SAVING TIPS

• *Consider bringing some food with you or making a stop at a supermarket.*

• *Pick up coupon booklets. These can offer 10%-off coupons and other bargains at eateries. This type of booklet is often distributed at the visitors' booth at the airport arrival area.*

• *Look for two-for-one specials.*

• *Look for early bird specials at some restaurants. Dining before 6pm can save money and it's smart with children.*

• *Look for free attractions. Remember, a stop doesn't necessarily have to be labeled "tourist attraction" to be fun and educational.*

INEXPENSIVE MOTELS ON THE STRIP
LA QUINTA (STRIP)
3782 Las Vegas Boulevard South, Tel. 702/739-7457 or 800/531-5900, Fax 702/736-1129, www.laquinta.com.

Rates: *$*
Amenities: *rollaway beds, complimentary breakfast*
Family-friendly facilities: *pool, kids under 18 stay free*

TRAVELODGE STRIP
2830 Las Vegas Boulevard South, Tel. 702/735-4222 or 800/578-7878, Fax 702/733-7695, www.travelodge.com.

Rates: *$-$$*
Amenities: *coffee maker in room, free parking, cable TV*
Family-friendly facilities: *outdoor heated pool, walking distance to Adventuredome at Circus Circus*

INEXPENSIVE MOTELS OFF THE STRIP
Off the Strip you'll find many motels that make good budget sense for families. Don't expect the extras or the atmosphere you'll find at the theme casino hotels, but you will find that these properties are very easy on the pocketbook and provide all the necessities. Many also offer free shuttles to the Strip so you can enjoy the expensive hotels to your heart's content.

AMERISUITES
4520 Paradise Road, Tel. 702/369-3366, www.amerisuites.com.

Rates: *$$-$$$*
Amenities: *voice mail, laundry service, business center, fitness center, shuttle*
Family-friendly facilities: *heated pool, separate rooms, free breakfast, kitchen facilities*

BEST WESTERN MCCARRAN INN
4970 Paradise Road, Tel. 702/798-5530 or 800/626-7575, Fax 702/798-7627, www.bestwestern.com.

Rates: *$-$$*
Amenities: *cable TV, courtesy shuttle to airport, MGM, and Strip*
Family-friendly facilities: *free Continental breakfast, pool, guest laundry, kids under 12 stay free, family suites available with separate sitting room and sleeper sofa*

COMFORT INN (CENTRAL)
211 E. Flamingo Road, Tel. 702/733-7800 or 800/634-6774, Fax 702/733-7353, www.comfortinn.com.

Rates: *$-$$*
Amenities: *bellman, free weekday newspaper*
Family-friendly facilities: *free Continental breakfast, pool*

COMFORT INN SOUTH
5075 Koval Lane, Tel. 702/736-3600, Fax 702/736-0726, www.comfortinn.com.

Rates: *$-$$*
Amenities: *cable TV*
Family-friendly facilities: *free Continental breakfast, kids stay free, pool*

DAYS INN - AIRPORT
5125 Swenson, Tel. 702/740-4040 or 800/329-7466, Fax 702/795-2325, www.days-inn.com.

Rates: *$-$$*
Amenities: *complimentary shuttle to MGM and airport, deli, ticket desk, convenience store, laundry, free newspaper*
Family-friendly facilities: *two pools, kids' game arcade*

This 183-room motel has a comfortable family feel. Its 24-hour complimentary shuttle to and from the airport is a real saver.

FAIRFIELD INN BY MARRIOTT

3850 Paradise Road, Tel. 702/791-0899, Fax 702/791-0899, www.marriott.com or www.fairfieldinn.com/LASFI.

Rates: *$-$$*
Amenities: *airport shuttle*
Family-friendly facilities: *complimentary Continental breakfast, outdoor pool*

This 129-room motel is just a mile from the Strip. It is a favorite with meeting travelers but also has features like the complimentary continental breakfast that make it a good choice for families.

HOWARD JOHNSON'S AIRPORT

5100 Paradise Road, Tel. 702/798-2777 or 800/634-6439, Fax 702/736-8295, www.hojo.com.

Rates: *$-$$*
Amenities: *24-hour complimentary airport shuttle, free transportation to MGM, walking distance to Thomas and Mack Events Center, small casino cocktail lounge*
Family-friendly facilities: *outdoor pool*

HOWARD JOHNSON – PLAZA

3111 West Tropicana Avenue, Tel. 702/798-1111 or 800/300-7389, Fax 702/798-7138, www.hojo.com.

Rates: *$-$$*
Amenities: *walk to Strip, slot machines*
Family-friendly facilities: *outdoor pool*

MOTEL 6 AT TROPICANA

195 E. Tropicana Avenue, Tel. 702/798-0728 or 800/466-8356, Fax 702/798-5657, www.motel6.com.

Rates: *$*
Amenities: *free movies, restaurant*
Family-friendly facilities: *kids stay free, outdoor pool*

PARKWAY INN

5201 S. Industrial Rd., Tel. 702/739-9513, Fax 702/739-7810.

Rates: *$*
Amenities: *cable TV, movie channels in rooms*
Family-friendly facilities: *swimming pool*

SUPER 8 MOTEL AT KOVAL

4250 Koval Lane, Tel. 702/794-0888 or 800/800/8000, Fax 702/794-3504. www.super8.com.

Rates: *$*
Amenities: *casino/game room, 24-hour shuttle*
Family-friendly facilities: *pool, rollaway beds are available for just $4, cribs for $2*

TRAVELODGE WEST SAHARA

1501 W. Sahara Avenue, Tel. 702/733-0001 or 800/578-7878, Fax 702/ 733-1571, www.travelodge.com.

Rates: *$-$$*
Amenities: *complimentary shuttle to Strip, restaurant, free newspaper*
Family-friendly facilities: *complimentary Continental breakfast, pool*

5. WHAT'S FOR DINNER?

GREAT PLACES TO EAT WITH KIDS

Las Vegas is increasingly adding fine dining restaurants, places where you can enjoy some of the world's best food and drink in an elegant atmosphere.

We're not going to cover those restaurants here. We know what families want. Burgers. Pizza. Buffets.

You're in good luck with the buffets. You've heard the stories of buffets that stretch like a desert highway, all the way to the horizon. Of prices that leave you plenty of money in the old vacation budget for whatever you choose (of course, the hosting casino hopes you'll spend it with them, but this is a book for families).

The famous Las Vegas buffet got its start in the early 1940s with the El Rancho Vegas Hotel. As the first hotel on the Las Vegas Strip, the hotel was looking for a way to keep customers in the joint after the second show. They came up with the Midnight Chuck Wagon Buffet and guests could have all they could eat for a dollar.

Today you won't find $1 buffets, but you will find good deals on food and massive selection to boot. There are often concessions to this orgy of inexpensive food, however: you may have to eat at certain hours to take advantage of the low buffet price, and you may have to stand in some long lines as well.

The buffet tradition is still going strong, though. At the Circus Circus Hotel-Casino, over 10,000 people a day are served buffet style (one day they did over 17,600 worth of plate filling!) Some hotels have decided to specialize with weekend champagne brunch buffets or theme buffets.

What's an average spread at a Vegas buffet? Look for about 45 selections.

RESTAURANT PRICES

How much will you have to spend on a dinner in Las Vegas? Often less than you might think. The buffets are generally a good deal and there are plenty of inexpensive eateries and food courts for families to enjoy as well.

We've given you this pricing guide for all restaurants:

$$$ – over $20 per person
$$ – $10-20 per person
$ – under $10 person
This figure includes an entree, drink, and gratuity.

HOTEL RESTAURANTS

With the size of Las Vegas's hotels, you could very well work up an appetite for a meal by walking from one end to the other. Whether you're staying at one of these hotels or just in to enjoy the fun or a show, we've arranged these restaurants by hotel. Each property has additional restaurants, but we felt these would be most popular with dining families:

BALLY'S CASINO RESORT
3645 Las Vegas Boulevard South, Tel. 702/739-4111 or 800/634-3434, Fax 702/739-4405, www.ballyslv.com.

Bally's Avenue Shoppes, *$*. This shopping arcade includes several fast food family options such as Sabarro's Italian Eatery and Stage Deli.

The Big Kitchen Buffet, *$$*. This buffet is huge even by Vegas standards. If you can only do one buffet while in town, this is the one.

CAESARS PALACE
3570 Las Vegas Boulevard South, Tel. 702/731-7110, Fax 702/731-7172, www.caesars.com.

Planet Hollywood, *$$*. It's not actually at Caesars but in the Forum Shops next door, but this eatery is worth a few extra steps for family fun. With its memorabilia-packed decor, this one is a sure pleaser with any movie buffs in the family. The menu's not bad either, with everything from burgers to shrimp to salads.

La Piazza Food Court, *$*. Families enjoy this food court, with nine outlets including a deli, pizza shop, Mexican restaurant, salad bar, and others.

Cafe Roma, *$-$$*. This eatery overlooks the casino and serves up a little bit of everything, from burgers to breakfast.

Palatium, *$$*. This buffet serves up an array of entrees with two carving stations, two dessert islands, and two frozen yogurt sundae buffets, a real winner with kids. Breakfast, lunch and dinner menus are served weekdays and on the weekends a brunch menu is offered.

CIRCUS CIRCUS

2880 Las Vegas Boulevard South, Tel. 702/734-0410 or 800/634-3450, Fax 702/734-0410, www.circuscircus.com.

Blue Iguana, *$$*. This restaurant serves up all sorts of Mexican dishes, from tacos to enchiladas. Open for dinner.

The Pink Pony, *$*. This 24-hour restaurant serves breakfast as well as burgers, dinner and desserts.

EXCALIBUR

3850 Las Vegas Boulevard South, Tel. 702/597-7777 or 800/937-7777, Fax 702/597-7040, www.excalibur-casino.com.

Nitro Grill, *$$*. In the footsteps of the Hard Rock Cafe and Planet Hollywood comes the Nitro Grill, a tribute to World Championship Wrestling (seriously). The WCW Nitro Grill is the world's first and it showcases the performers, no we mean athletes, of the wrestling world. Not surprisingly, you'll find plenty of meat and potatoes here as well as souvenir merchandise. If you've got a wrestling lover in the family, this is a fun place for a meal.

Round Table Buffet, *$-$$*. Looking for an all-you-can-eat experience? Then you'll find breakfast, lunch and dinner at this expansive buffet. For dinner, there's a roast beef carving station.

Sherwood Forest Café, *$-$$*. This 24-hour eatery serves up a full menu of coffee shop items, including breakfast, lunch and dinner. For dinner, the cafe has several Chinese specialties.

Village Food Court, *$*. When you're in the mood for a quick meal, this food court has something for everyone: McDonald's, ice cream, pretzels, doughnuts, you name it.

Tournament of Kings, *$$$*. This dinner show features jousters, wizards, dragons, and plenty of medieval atmosphere. Kids will like the food service, too – it's all enjoyed without cutlery for an authentic medieval dining experience. Tickets are $36.95. Dinner shows are presented twice daily at 6pm and 8:30pm. For reservations or information, call *702/597-7600*.

HOLIDAY INN BOARDWALK

3750 Las Vegas Boulevard South, Tel. 702/735-1167 or 800/465-4329, Fax 702/739-8152, www.hiboardwalk.com.

Caffe Boardwalk, *$-$$*. This main dining room is open daily for breakfast, lunch and dinner.

The Deli, *$*. This 24-hour eatery has plenty of kid favorites like Coney Island hot dogs.

Surf Buffet, *$*. Unlike most buffets, this one is open 24 hours and has American food as well as Italian, Mexican, and Asian specialties, all enjoyed in a beach-themed eatery.

Coney Island Ice Cream Parlor, *$*. Hey, it's your vacation, remember! What's one scoop of ice cream?

IMPERIAL PALACE

3535 Las Vegas Boulevard South, Tel. 702/731-3311 or 800/634-6441, Fax 702/735-8578, www.imperialpalace.com.

You've got several choices in this large hotel, everything from fast food to buffets:

Pizza Palace, *$*. It's pizza time! You'll also find many Italian dishes at this fifth floor restaurant which is open daily from 11am.

Imperial Buffet, *$*. This buffet offers a special Prime Rib Champagne Dinner daily from 5pm-10pm for just $9.45 or $5 for kids. On weekends, there's a champagne brunch from 8am-3pm for $8.45 (kids $5). Breakfast and lunch buffets are also available for $7.45 ($4.50 for kids).

Emperor's Buffet, *$*. This third floor restaurant has a sprawling array of dishes. A breakfast buffet is available from 7am-11:30am for $6.25 (kids $4.25); lunch buffet is served 11:30am-5pm for $7.50 (kids $5.49); dinner buffet is 5pm-10pm for $8.50 (kids $5.99).

Burger Palace, *$*. More in the mood for a burger? You'll find it, along with chicken or fish sandwiches and snacks at this third floor restaurant.

Betty's Diner, *$*. Located on the main floor in the shopping arcade, this is a good place to grab snacks.

Hawaiian Hot Luau, *$$$*. Available only from April through October on Tuesday and Thursday evenings, this poolside event is a fun combination of dinner and show. The evening starts at 6:30pm with an evening of Polynesian seafood (served at a buffet), unlimited Mai Tai and Pina Coladas as well as non-alcoholic fruit punch, and music and dance with an island flair. The area is lit with torches but the real "lighting" comes with a fire knife dance. Kids can even take part in hula lessons and a sing-a-long. Characters from the hotel's "Legends in Concert" show (above) also drop by. Reservations are required for the luau. Stop by the Show Reservation booth on the first floor or the Shangri-La pool bar, or call *702/ 794-3261*.

LUXOR

3900 Las Vegas Boulevard South, Tel. 702/262-4000 or 800/288-1000.

Pharoah's Pheast Buffet, *$*. Yes, it's a feast all right. Designed to look like it's set in an archaeological dig, this fun buffet has plenty of options including a variety of international cuisines. The food is nothing to write home about, but it's lots of fun for the whole family.

Food Court, *$*. Sometimes it just has to be fast food; when the kids need food now, you'll find hot dogs, ice cream and pizza in this food court.

MANDALAY BAY

3950 Las Vegas Boulevard South, Tel. 702/632-7777 or 877/632-7000, www.mandalaybay.com.

Bay Side Buffet, *$$*. This buffet has a nice view of the watergardens plus plenty of dining options, whether you're visiting for breakfast, lunch or dinner.

Raffles Cafe, *$-$$*. This 24-hour cafe has views of the "beach" and a menu that includes a little bit of everything.

MGM GRAND HOTEL AND CASINO

3799 Las Vegas Boulevard South,, 800/929-1111 or 702/891-7777, www.mgmgrand.com.

Rainforest Cafe, *$$*. This 500-seat restaurant will have kids feeling welcome. The restaurant's theme is carried out from its decor to its menu. Look for an animated gorilla family, misting waterfalls, a 10,000 gallon saltwater aquarium, animatronic elephants, simulated tropical rainstorms... the whole works except for Tarzan. Kids will have fun with the menu names like "Rumble in the Jungle Turkey Pita" or "Gorillas in the Mist Cheesecake." Kids under age 12 can order off the "Rainforest Rascals" menu.

Food Court, *$*. You'll find all the fast food necessities here.

Cabana Grill, *$*. This poolside cafe is just open during the warm weather months, but it's a fun place to have lunch of pizza, burgers, or sandwiches while the kids romp in the pool area.

MGM Grand Buffet, *$-$$*. This buffet always offers eight different entrees and the menu changes daily in case you want to eat here more than once during your stay. During the brunch shift, you'll find ham and turkey carving stations; the dinner buffet always includes chilled shrimp. Brunch is served 7am-2:30pm for $9.50, kids under 12 $5.95; dinner is served 4:30-10pm for $13.95, kids $7.95. Kids under age 4 eat without charge.

MIRAGE
3400 Las Vegas Boulevard South, Tel. 702/791-7111 or 800/627-6667, Fax 702/791-7446, www.themirage.com.

Buffet, *$$*. The Mirage buffet is a sprawling thing to behold with over 150 items. Breakfast is served 7am-10:45am, lunch from 11am-2:45pm, and dinner from 3pm-10pm. On Sundays, they offer a champagne brunch from 8am-3pm.

MONTE CARLO
3770 Las Vegas Boulevard South, Tel. 702/730-7777 or 800/311-8999, Fax 702/730-7200, www.monte-carlo.com/

Market City, *$$*. This eatery serves up Southern Italian dishes, starting with an antipasto bar and continuing through to pizzas, pastas, and plenty of other selections.

Buffet, *$$*. This buffet is fun for its exhibition chefs. The buffet has too many dishes to count and it's all served beneath Moroccan arches.

NEW YORK-NEW YORK HOTEL AND CASINO

3790 Las Vegas Boulevard, Tel. 702/740-6969 or 800/693-6763, Fax 702/891-5285, www.nynyhotelcasino.com.

New York-New York has many restaurants that serve everything from fine food to, predictably enough, hot dogs.

America, *$-$$*. This 24-hour eatery specializes in, you guessed it, American food. With a huge map of the states, the restaurant features a menu that has dishes from around the country (accompanied by beers from around the nation as well).

Coney Island Pavillion, *$*. Grab a Nathan's Hot Dog or some ice cream at this fun eatery.

RIO SUITES HOTEL AND CASINO

3700 W. Flamingo Road, Tel. 702/252-7777 or 800/752-9746, Fax 702/253-6090, www.playrio.com.

Carnival World Buffet, *$$*. This buffet truly does offer a selection of world cuisines. Asian cuisines, Italian, and even South American fill the all-you-can-eat offerings here.

Village Seafood Buffet, *$$*. If you've got a seafood lover in the family, this all-you-can-eat extravaganza is a sure winner.

Star Deli and Bakery, *$*. Sometimes when you're traveling, there's nothing better than a simple sandwich or a fresh bagel.

RIVIERA

2901 Las Vegas Boulevard South, Tel. 702/734-5110 or 800/634-6753, Fax 702/794-9451, www.theriviera.com

Mardi Gras Food Court, *$*. When you're traveling with kids, sometimes you just have to fall back on favorites like Burger King and Pizza Hut. You'll find them here.

Kady's Coffee Shop, *$*. This cafe is open 24 hours for breakfast, lunch or dinner.

STRATOSPHERE

2000 Las Vegas Boulevard South, Tel. 702/380-7777 or 800/998-6937, Fax 702/383-5334, www.stratlv.com.

Roxy's Diner, $-$$. This 24-hour diner serves up favorites like burgers and shakes.

Montana's Steakhouse, $$-$$$. This steakhouse is casual and family-friendly.

TREASURE ISLAND

3300 Las Vegas Boulevard South, Tel. 702/894-7111 or 800/944-7444, Fax 702/894-7446, www.treasureisland.com.

Buccaneer Bay Club, $$$. This exclusive restaurant is a good one for a "dress up" night or if you're celebrating a special occasion during your stay. The restaurant overlooks Buccaneer Bay Village and the sea battle but if you want a seat with a view, plan to make reservations. The eatery is open daily 5pm-10:30pm, and note that children under the age of five aren't permitted in the restaurant. Bring along dressy clothes for this special eatery.

Black Spot Grille, *$-$$*. Looking for something more casual? Then the answer just might be the Black Spot Grille, with its menu of burgers, pastas, salads, and wood-fired pizzas. This casual eatery is open 11-11 daily (until 12:30am Friday and Saturday).

RESTLESS RESTAURANT DINING

This is a warning: Las Vegas restaurants can be packed. Service may not be speedy. You will wait. Your kids will wait.

And they may not wait gracefully. Even the most patient diners can become restless. Here are a few tips for dealing with young (and not so young) restless diners:

• consider buffets. The buffet is a Vegas institution, stretching like a desert highway and filled with every kind of entree under the sun. This is a great option for families, for price, selection, and time.

• bring activities. The wait for food is a perfect time to catch up on postcard writing, travel diaries, and other "desk" activities for schoolage children.

• use the time to discuss your day and plan the next day's activities. Go around the table and ask everyone what their favorite activity that day was. What has been their favorite food? Their favorite attraction?

RESTAURANTS NOT LOCATED IN HOTELS
ALL-STAR CAFE

3785 Las Vegas Blvd. South in Showcase Mall by MGM Grand, Tel. 702/795-8326, $$.

Like a sports version of the Hard Rock Cafe, this memorabilia-filled eatery contains sports items from big names like Tiger Woods and Wayne Gretsky. The menu is all-American with burgers and hot dogs that are sure to please young travelers.

DIVE!

3200 Las Vegas Blvd. in Fashion Show Mall, Tel. 702/369-DIVE, $$.

This theme restaurant, devised by Steven Spielburg, makes you feel like you're down in a submarine. Kids can play with the periscopes or check out the portholes while waiting for the food (and, yes, they do have sub sandwiches).

HARD ROCK CAFE

4475 Paradise Road, Tel. 702/733-8400. $$.

If you've got a music lover in the family, then Hard Rock is a must. It's filled with all kinds of rock 'n roll memorabilia (and sells overpriced T-shirts) with the usual Hard Rock menu of burgers, salads, and other lunch fare. Budget some time here; there can be a wait.

HIPPO AND THE WILD BUNCH

4503 Paradise Rd., Tel. 702/731-5446. $$.

Who wouldn't love a restaurant whose staff buzzes around on roller skates? This kids' favorite is filled with balloons, animal sculptures, music, and plenty of fun. The menu includes burgers, pizza, and some Southwestern dishes.

6. WHAT ARE WE DOING NEXT?

THE BEST FAMILY ATTRACTIONS IN LAS VEGAS

Las Vegas definitely has plenty of attractions to hold family interest, from rollercoasters to volcanoes to star travel. We've divided this chapter by type of activity.

FUN & FANTASY

There's no place else like Las Vegas to bring out the fun and the fantasy of a destination. Here you'll find fanciful attractions that transport you to King Arthur's Court, the days of ancient Rome, the pyramids of Egypt, and more.

Kids love the **Dragon Battle at Excalibur**, *3850 Las Vegas Boulevard South, Tel. 702/597-7777.* The fight takes place every hour between dusk and midnight, weather permitting. The battle is complete with a fire breathing dragon and takes place in the moat outside the hotel.

While you're at Excalibur, don't miss the free show of the **Court Jesters**. These strolling entertainers perform every 45 minutes from 10-10 daily and are great fun with their jokes and juggling.

FUN & FREE

Who says you get what you pay for? In Las Vegas, there's a full slate of activities that don't cost a dime (or a chip). You won't need to reach for the wallet for this family fun:

Caesar's Fountain Show (Fun and Fantasy, above)

Circus, Circus Circus (Circus, below)

Clown Factory (see Factory Tours, below)

Court Jesters at Excalibur (Fun and Fantasy, above)

Dragon Battle at Excalibur (Fun and Fantasy, above)

Fountains at Bellagio (Fun and Fantasy, below)

Fremont Street Experience (Fun and Fantasy, below)

Lion Habitat, MGM Grand (Animals, below)

Lost City of Atlantis, Forum Shops at Caesars (Fun and Fantasy, below)

Masquerade Show in the Sky, Rio (Fun and Fantasy, below)

Mystic Falls Park, Sam's Town (Fun and Fantasy, below)

Pirate Ship Battle, Treasure Island (Fun and Fantasy, below)

Volcano, The Mirage (Fun and Fantasy, below)

White Tiger Habitat, The Mirage (Animals, below)

Masquerade Village, *Rio Suites Hotel and Casino, 3700 W. Flamingo Rd., Tel. 702/252-7777,* has all the fun of carnival in a fantasy setting. The action takes place with floats that are suspended from the ceiling and a parade above the floor of the casino. The Masquerade Show in the Sky consists of four themed parades throughout the day designed to give the atmosphere of New Orleans's Mardi Gras, the Venice Carnival, Rio's Carnivale, and a village street party. Join in the fun and ride a float!

Pirate Battle, *Treasure Island, 3300 Las Vegas Boulevard South, Tel. 702/894-7111,* has to be seen to be believed. We recommend that you get here early (the first time we saw the show, we arrived over half an hour early and still didn't have a good place to stand and watch the show. Arrive early to stand next to the rail and expect large crowds.) The free show takes place in front of Treasure Island starting at 4pm. In front of the hotel, a bay village described in Robert Lewis Stevenson's novel *Treasure Island* comes to life with a battle between a pirate ship and the H.M.S. *Sir Francis Drake*.

Just next door, The Mirage has a crowd-drawing show of its own thanks to the volcano! Yes, it's a live **Volcano** *at the Mirage, 3400 Las Vegas Boulevard South, Tel. 702/791-7111 or 800/627-6667, Fax 702/791-7446, www.themirage.com*. Just outside the hotel stands a man-made waterfall with a volcano that "explodes" every fifteen minutes during the evening hours. Molten "lava" pours from the volcano and cascades down the waterfall to delight the shoulder-to-shoulder crowds that circle this unique attraction.

Ever seen a talking statue? Then head to the **Fountain Show**, *Forum Shops at Caesars Palace, 3500 Las Vegas Boulevard South, Tel. 702/893-4800*. This free show occurs every hour on the hour between 11am and 10pm. It's a quick show (just seven or eight minutes) so don't be late. The event features moving Roman statues, special lighting effects, and more.

Or travel to a park inside a hotel at the **Sunset Stampede**, *Sam's Town Hotel & Gambling Hall, 5111 Boulder Hwy., Tel. 702/456-7777*. This show brings "Mystic Falls Park" to life with a laser light and water show. It's also free and is performed four times per day.

It's pure fantasy at the **Bellagio Fountains**, *The Bellagio, 3600 Las Vegas Boulevard South, Tel. 702/693-7444, www.bellagiolasvegas.com*. These fountains are beautifully choreographed, using all types of music as a backdrop for the 1000 feet of fountains that shoot up to 240 feet in the air.

Carnaval Court, *3475 Las Vegas Boulevard South, Tel. 702/369-5000 or 800/427-7247, Fax 702/369-5008, www. harrahs.lv.com.* This outdoor area has the feel of a street fair. Kids can get hot dogs and pretzels from the vendors from 10am - 8pm daily; during the spring and summer months live entertainment fills the piazza with fun.

Downtown travelers can enjoy the $70 million **Fremont Street Experience**. This unique 175,700-square-foot light and sound show is a pedestrian experience located right on Fremont Street. A 90-foot tall canopy covers four acres of the street. Over two million lights dance across the canopy in a six-minute every hour after dark.

THEME PARKS

Back in the early 90s when Vegas thought they'd give the family market a serious roll of the dice, MGM Grand Adventures was built as a serious theme park. Well, as the family market became less of a focus for the glittery city, the theme park trimmed back some but the fun remains. You'll find several theme parks in town, all worth at least a few hours.

MGM GRAND ADVENTURES

MGM Grand, 3799 Las Vegas Boulevard South, 702/891-7979.

MGM Grand's theme park is divided into six themed areas. The best deal is the wristband, which gives you unlimited rides throughout the park on everything except the SkyScreamer (more on that in a minute) for $12. The park hours change seasonally so check in before making your plans.

The park has all speeds of rides, from tame to tortuous. If you've got a roller coaster buff in the family, head to the **Lightning Bolt**. This outdoor roller coaster goes over the Grand Canyon

Rapids and up to heights of 70 feet. Tamer fun is found on **Over the Edge**, a log ride that takes you through a "saw mill" then takes a 42-foot drop.

Tamer still is **Grand Canyon Rapids**. A popular ride on hot summer days, this raft ride bounces past a Wild West shootout (and even past coin-operated water bombs operated by wicked spectators on warm weather days).

Young children enjoy **Les Bumper Boats**. You can drive the little bumper boats and it's lots of fun for the family. Bumper cars are found at Parisian Taxis, all set on a "Paris street."

Another favorite family ride is **Pedalin' Paddleboats**. You'll have control over your own paddleboat on the lake (and get a good view of the SkyScreamer).

All right, more on that **SkyScreamer**. This isn't one of those rides we personally tested, but for those you game for a heart-pumping, adrenaline rush of a ride, here's the rundown. SkyScreamer is called the world's largest Skycoaster. You (alone or with one or two other flyers, depending on the ticket you purchased) are whisked up 220 feet in the air. You pull your own ripcord and start a free fall that's clocked at up to 70 mph. (Now you see why we didn't experience this one first hand.) The cost of the SkyScreamer is $35 if you do it by yourself, $30 per person if you go with one other rider, and $25 per person if three of you are crazy enough to take this ride. The ticket price includes general admission to the park.

The park also has plenty of live, family oriented entertainment (a good option on hot summer days when it's time for a little rest). **Pirates Cove** has an excellent Dueling Pirates Stunt show, complete with a large pirate ship in a lagoon. **Star Steppin' Stage** on

French Street and **Show Place Junction** on New Orleans Street both feature live entertainment.

The park also has several indoor theaters (good places to beat the heat, summer visitors!) **Magic Screen Theatre** and **Gold Rush Theatre** offer changing shows, so check the day's schedule.

Other attractions at the park include arcades and family-friendly eateries with everything from pizza to ice cream. You'll also find strollers for rent at the park's Canterbury Square (there are also lockers here if you're ready to stow that diaper bag). If there's a boo-boo, check with first aid in the Asian Village.

ADVENTUREDOME AT CIRCUS CIRCUS

2880 Las Vegas Boulevard South, Tel. 702/794-3939, www.adventuredome.com.

If you came to Vegas a few years ago, you might have heard about the Grand Slam Canyon at the Circus Circus. Well, today that five-acre theme park is called the Adventuredome at Circus Circus, and it's filled with family-friendly rides and games. There's a roller coaster, laser tag, animated dinosaurs, an arcade, and water rides. The whole five-acre park is set under glass, maintains a constant 72 degrees (perfect for a rainy day or one where it's just too hot to budge outside), and is considered the largest indoor theme park in the country.

The cost for an unlimited ride pass is $12.95 for kids 33 to 47 inches tall and $16.95 for travelers over 48 inches high. Kids under 33 inches tall come in for free. The hours vary by season so check with the hotel before making your plans.

What's the appeal of the Adventuredome? Here's a rundown of the top rides:

•**The Canyon Blaster**. Circus Circus calls this the world's largest indoor double-loop, double-corkscrew roller coaster in the country. It's for real thrill seekers, buzzing around at 55 mph and pulling both positive and negative G-forces. Not for us but teens usually love it.

Restriction: riders must be 48 inches tall.

•**Rim Runner.** Ready to get wet? You're in the right place. You'll board a boat on this ride for a float through caverns (watch out for the dinosaurs!) and some pretty areas before you take a drop off a 60-foot waterfall. If this one's too wild for you (hey, you can always say you would do it, but you can't because of the kids), make a stop at the viewing area to see the boats drop off the cliff.

Restriction: riders must be 48 inches tall.

•**Fun House Express.** This IMAX Motion Simulator was specially designed for Circus Circus and uses computer images along with motion to send simulate a fun house ride.

Restriction: riders must be 42 inches tall.

•**Lazer Blast Laser Tag**: Ready for laser tag? You'll see by the glow of black light as you join a team and participate in a five-minute game in this 7500-square-foot facility. Participants wear a special vest and use laser guns to wipe out the opposition.

Restriction: game participants must be 42 inches tall.

•**Road Runner**: a ride for the whole family!

•**Xtreme Zone**: This attraction combines wall climbing and trampolining!

• **Thunderbirds**: Another ride for everyone! Kids board model 1920 airplanes and buzz around.

• **Drifters**: Don't want to fly a plane? How about a hot air balloon? This Ferris wheel is made up of hot air balloon cars and is fun for all riders.

• **Canyon Cars**: Hold on, it's time for the bumper cars! (And you're not even out on Las Vegas Boulevard!)

• **Cliffhangers**: Younger kids like the tunnels and balls at this playscape.

• **Inverter**: OK, the thrill rides aren't over yet. This stomach churner (literally) flips 360 degrees, has a constant G force, and isn't for everyone.

• **Miniature golf**: With a full 18 holes, this is a fun family activity.

WET 'N WILD

2601 Las Vegas Boulevard South, Tel. 702/734-0088, www.wetnwildlv.com.

Perfect for the heat of Las Vegas, **Wet 'n Wild** combines the fun of a theme park with the cooling rides of a water park. Kids will find several hours worth of cool fun here.

The park has several rides that are at a pace that can be enjoyed by the whole family. Our favorite is the 1/4-mile-long **Lazy River**, where you can hop aboard an inner tube and take a luxurious slow float down the "river" beneath swaying palm trees. Another good family ride is the **Surf Lagoon**, which gives the feel of ocean waves in a pool that ranges from deep to tot-size, just two inches deep. Kids (unless they get dizzy easily) enjoy the **Willy Willy**, which is called the world's first hydra-hurricane. The aquatic funnel takes riders in a circle at a pace of 10 miles per hour.

The park also has a special kids' section for young visitors, with miniature versions of the larger slides. This kids' section also includes a playground with child-sized beach chairs and tables and it's all overseen by professional lifeguards.

The park also has plenty of thrill rides, very popular with the pre-teen and teen set. The **Black Hole**, like its name suggests, is a black tower with spaghetti-like tubes descending from it; two riders per raft are shot down the 500-foot-long tubes by jets of water for a quick, dark ride. **Banzai Banzai** is another fast, but open air ride; participants hop aboard a sled and zip down the water coaster before skipping out across the pool like a tossed stone.

Blue Niagra is similar to the Black Hole, riders enter black tubes that twist and promise a scary ride. **Bomb Bay** turns riders into human "bombs" dropped down a nearly vertical slide. The fastest water chute at the park (and, according to Wet 'n Wild, in the world) is **Der Stuka**®. This chute drops riders down a nearly vertical slide for 76 feet. For something a little more tame, try the **Raging Rapids**, similar to a whitewater river rafting experience.

And, appropriate for Las Vegas, there's the **Royal Flush**. Riders can pick between an enclosed bowl or an uncovered bowl. The flush occurs when the rider is swept into the chute and spun around the bowl (at up to 45 mph!) before finally being flushed into the pool below.

The park is open seasonally (and the pools are heated when the weather necessitates). Hours fluctuate by month; the park is open late April through September. During the summer months, look for the park to be open 10am-8pm from Sunday through Thursday and until 10pm on Friday and Saturday, but call ahead for exact hours. Admission price is $25.95 for visitors over 48 inches tall and $19.95 for visitors under 48 inches. Children under age three are admitted free.

WET 'N WILD TIP

A good way to save money at the park is to bring a picnic and some drinks (although glass containers and alcoholic beverages are out).

GOOD VIEWS

With its spectacular lights, Las Vegas is a beautiful city to view at night, although daytime views can be spectacular as well, overlooking the surrounding desert. There are several good observation points:

How about a ride up the Eiffel Tower? Thanks to the **Eiffel Tower Experience**, *Paris Las Vegas, Tel. 877/796-2096, www.paris-lv.com*, it's easy. You'll take a quick elevator ride up to the observation deck; the view is great. The ride costs $8.

The highest observation point is the **Stratosphere Tower**, *Stratosphere, 2000 Las Vegas Boulevard South, Tel. 702/380-7777 or 800/998-6937, Fax 702/383-5334, www.stratlv.com.* The tallest building west of the Mississippi River and the tallest freestanding observation tower in the US, this 1149-foot tower is home to two observation decks. On the 108th level, the **Pepsi Cola Indoor Observation Deck** is the best choice for anyone who's a little leery of being out in the open at such a height. It's 857 feet above the ground and climate controlled. There's a snack bar at the deck as well as two gift shops. On the next level, the **Pepsi Cola Outdoor Observation Deck** is located a 869 feet above the ground and it's got all the sensation of being outside at such a height. This level also has the added advantage of being a good place to watch the rides on the Big Shot and the High Roller (see below).

The observation decks are open from 10am-1am Sunday through Thursday, 10am-2am Friday and Saturday. Tower admission is $6 for adults and $3 for Nevada residents with a photo ID or for kids ages 4-12 or seniors over 55. Kids under 4 are admitted free of charge.

RIDES

What's the wildest ride in town? It's got to be found at the **Stratosphere**, *2000 Las Vegas Boulevard South, Tel. 702/380-7777, www.stratlv.com*. Here you can take your choice between the **Big Shot** and the **High Roller**. The High Roller is located on the 112th level of the mega-tower. At 909 feet, the ride zips and whizzes its way around the tower at a speed of 30 miles per hour.

Even wilder is the **Big Shot**. Located above the High Roller, this ride quickly elevates 16 passengers 160 feet in 2.5 seconds, then drops them back down to the launch pad to achieve zero G's.

Can't stomach either? There's also an **observation area** on the open 109th floor observation deck.

Both rides are open 10am-1am Sunday through Thursday and until 2am on Friday and Saturday. The High Roller tickets are $5 and the Big Shot costs $6 (or buy a tower admission and ride combo for $9 for the High Roller and $10 for the Big Shot). Restrictions: riders must be 48 inches tall.

It's a bird, it's a plane...no, it's a rollercoaster. **The Manhattan Express®**, *New York - New York Hotel & Casino, 3790 Las Vegas*

Boulevard S., Tel. 702/740-6969, www.nynyhotelcasino.com, whips around the hotel in a series of twists and dives and reaches speeds up to 67 mph. Check out the website for a virtual version of this rollercoaster that puts the roll back in the coaster. The cost of the ride is $8. **Restrictions**: riders must be 54 inches or taller.

Looking for another roller coaster? Head over to the Sahara to the new **Speed – The Ride**, *Sahara, 2535 Las Vegas Boulevard South, Tel. 702/737-2111.* This monster of a ride tosses riders around what seems to be a runaway roller coaster, buzzing right on through the hotel marquee. The short ride costs $8; the ride runs from 10am-10pm daily and until midnight on Friday and Saturday nights. **Restrictions**: riders must be 52 inches tall.

A big hit with families is **Star Trek: The Experience**, *Las Vegas Hilton, 3000 Paradise Road, Tel. 702/732-5111 or 800/732-7117, www.startrekexp.com.* This attraction (a joint project between the hotel and Paramount Parks) is a sure winner with Star Trek buffs of all ages (and even those who don't know the popular TV series and movies will love the special effects). The venture includes a simulator ride, interactive video and virtual reality stations, a themed restaurant, and retail shopping. The casino includes three "windows" into space which project changing panoramic views and create the illusion of orbiting Earth from sunrise to sunset.

Star Trek buffs will love the **History of the Future Museum**, the largest permanent collection of Star Trek memorabilia in the world. There are plenty of costumes and accessories on display from the shows.

The centerpiece of the attraction, though, is the **Voyage through Space**. After a look around the museum, you'll enter the Starfleet Gallery Room to be beamed aboard a replica of the Starfleet Enterprise bridge. Escorts then take you to the shuttle bay to board a shuttlecraft and take a simulated ride through the universe to a space station and television screens create an illusion of space flight. Visitors assume the identity of a Starfleet or alien crew member.

COMBO RIDE TICKETS

You can buy a combination ticket for Star Trek: The Experience, Madame Tussaud's Celebrity Encounter, Race for Atlantis, and the Stratosphere's Big Shot for $37.95.

Or would you prefer a gondola ride through Venice? Then head over to the **Gondola Rides**, *The Venetian, Tel. 877/857-1861.* For $10 for adults, $5 for kids 12 and under, you can take a relaxing ride on a gondola. You'll need cash for this excursion. Reservation are required as well but can be made only at the loading dock in St. Marks Square for rides that day.

An easier ride with shorter lines is the **Menagerie Carousel**, *The Meadows Mall, 4300 Meadow Ln., Tel. 702/878-4849.* This fun carousel is filled with animal shapes and the price is right (just 50 cents a ride).

VIRTUAL RIDES & SPECIAL THEATERS

These rides are just our speed. Thanks to supersized screens and/or specially designed movie seats, you'll have all the sensation of thrill rides but all the safety of a movie.

Hold on and get ready to move and see a movie at the same time. The **Magic Motion Rides**, *Excalibur, 3850 Las Vegas Boulevard South, Tel. 702/597-7777,* combine a 70mm film experience with mechanical seats that keep you leaning and diving in sync with the movie. The shows are fairly short so kids with brief attention spans will be OK, but this can be a little scary for some young ones. The rides run from 10am to midnight Monday through Thursday and until 1 am on Friday, 9am to 1 am on Saturday, and 9 am to midnight on Sunday. The cost is $3 per ride.

Restrictions: riders must be 42 inches tall.

Cinema Ride, *The Forum Shops at Caesar's Palace, 3500 Las Vegas Boulevard South, Tel. 702/369-4008,* is a good choice for those looking for the excitement of a thrill ride but with the assurance of a movie's safety. These are 3-D simulator thrill rides that give you the sensation of flying along in a roller coaster, a spaceship, a submarine, or other exciting vessels but all from the safety of your specially designed theater seat. Tickets are $9.50 for adults, $6.75 for kids 12 and under.

Restrictions: Riders must be at least 42 inches tall.

Two 3-D theaters are found at **Sahara Speedworld**, *Sahara, 2535 Las Vegas Boulevard South, Tel. 702/737-2111.* The cost is $3; the facility is open 10am-midnight daily.

At **Luxor**, *3900 Las Vegas Boulevard South, Tel. 800/288-1000,* you can visit the first IMAX theater in Las Vegas. This theater hosts a variety of shows specially designed for the seven-story screen. Cost is $8.95; call for show times.

Just down the street, the world's first giant-screen IMAX 3D motion simulator ride, **Race for Atlantis**, *Forum Shops at Caesars Palace, Tel. 877/427-7243.* Riders are outfitted with a 3D electronic headset with a personal sound system and liquid crystal shutters synchronized with an infrared signal from the IMAX projector.

The Race for Atlantis gives the illusion of a fantasy world where visitors watch Neptune battle a sea dragon. The cost is $8.

Restrictions: Riders must be at least 42 inches tall.

Theaters of Sensation, *Venetian Resort Hotel Casino, Grand Canal Shoppes, 3377 Las Vegas Boulevard South, Tel. 702/733-0545,* is a 3-D motion ride. The theater features five different films that rotate between two screens. The films include a gondola ride (a good choice if the lines are too long for the hotel's gondola rides!), a trip through time to King Tut's Tomb (that seems to be a popular theme in this town), and others. Combination tickets are available for four films or two films, each lasting just 10 minutes. The rides are open from 10am-11pm (and to midnight on Friday and Saturday nights).

Restrictions: riders must be 48 inches tall (except for the underwater ride with no motion). The cost is $9 for adults for one ride ($7 for kids).

Sahara Speedworld, *Sahara, 2535 Las Vegas Boulevard South, Tel. 702/737-21111,* lets kids try their luck behind the wheel of a virtual 3/4-scale Indy-style car for a virtual reality race. This $15-million, 40,000-square-foot virtual reality attraction gives the illusion of racing on the half oval at the Las Vegas Motor Speedway. The cost is $8; the arcade is open 10am-midnight daily.

Restrictions: riders must be 42 inches tall for the virtual reality rides, 48 inches tall for the cars.

RACEWAYS

Racers, start your engines and head to one of Las Vegas's kart tracks. The **Las Vegas Mini Gran Prix**, *1401 N. Rainbow Boulevard, Tel. 702/259-7000,* has several sizes of cars (including kiddie karts).

The cost is $4 per ride and the facility is open 10am-11pm daily (and until midnight on Friday and Saturday nights).

Restrictions: age 16 and older for Grand Prix; riders must be 54 inches tall for go-carts.

At the **Scandia Family Center**, *2900 Sirius Ave., Tel. 702/364-0070*, kids can race "Lil' Indy" cars or enjoy something tamer like mini golf, the pitching machines, or bumper boats. Open 10am-11pm daily (and until midnight on Friday and Saturday nights).

Restrictions: riders must be 54 inches tall for the raceway; 46 inches tall for the boats. The cost is $15.95 for an all-day pass with 10 arcade/batting tokens and unlimited raceway, golf, and boats.

Don't want the kids behind the wheel just yet? Then check out the **Sahara Speedworld**, *Sahara, 2535 Las Vegas Boulevard South, Tel. 702/737-21111*. Here kids get into a 3/4-scale Indy-style car for a virtual reality race. This $15-million, 40,000-square-foot virtual reality attraction gives the illusion of racing on the half oval at the Las Vegas Motor Speedway. The cost is $8; the arcade is open 10am-midnight daily.

Restrictions: riders must be 42 inches tall for the virtual reality rides, 48 inches tall for the cars.

MINIATURE GOLF
Putt-putt is always a fun family activity. At **Scandia Family Fun Center**, *2900 Sirius Ave., Tel. 702/364-0070*, you can take your choice from three 18-hole courses.

ARCADES

When you hear Gameworks, you may think of arcade games, but this entertainment center has a lot more. **Gameworks**, *Showcase Mall, 3785 Las Vegas Boulevard South, Tel. 702/432-4263,* is home to the Sega Power Sled with three sleds that riders steer (yes, even in a town that doesn't see snow); you'll also find what's called the world's tallest free-standing rock-climbing structure here. When you get hungry, there's a restaurant and some snack bars here. Gameworks is open 10 am to 4 am daily.

At Luxor, you'll find **Games of the Gods**, *3900 Las Vegas Boulevard South, Tel. 800/288-1000,* especially known for its interactive games. You can take a ride on a virtual rollercoaster in Maxflight VR2002 or race against seven other drivers in an Indy 500 simulator. There's even a simulated powerboat race where you buzz through the waterways of Japan, Russia, England or New York. Cost is $5.

Restrictions: riders must be 42 inches tall.

At New York-New York, the theme continues with **Coney Island Emporium**, *New York Hotel & Casino, 3790 Las Vegas Boulevard S., Tel. 702/740-6969.* It's all set against the backdrop of the summer resort and has plenty of arcade fun including interactive laser tag, virtual reality games, bumper cars, and a shooting gallery.

This arcade has some special rules, ones we think are a good move to keep the arcades safe for children. Children under the age of 18, unaccompanied by a parent, legal guardian or responsible adult over the age of 21, are prohibited from the arcade during these hours: Sunday - Thursday, after 10 p.m.; Friday, Saturday & Nevada School Holidays, after 12 midnight; and Memorial Day - Labor Day, after 12 midnight.

Circus Circus is home to the **Carnival Midway**, *2880 Las Vegas Boulevard South, Tel. 800/634-3450,* filled with midway games as well as an electronic arcade with almost 200 games. The midway is open 10am-midnight (until 1am on Friday and Saturday).

At **Sahara Speedworld**, *Sahara, 2535 Las Vegas Boulevard South, Tel. 702/737-21111,* riders can take their seats in a 3/4-scale Indy-style car for a virtual reality race. The cost is $8; the arcade is open 10am-midnight daily.

Restrictions: riders must be 42 inches tall for the virtual reality rides, 48 inches tall for the cars.

BIG TOP ACTION!

The **Circus** at *Circus Circus, 2880 Las Vegas Boulevard South, Tel. 702/734-0410 or 800/634-3450,* is the best deal in town. You can watch different acts every half hour from 11am-midnight daily. Jugglers, acrobats, and performers from around the world make up the show, which brings in new performers frequently. The Circus is also home to the Midway, an arcade with both electronic and old-fashioned games; see more about it in Arcades, above.

LION FACTS

*The **MGM Grand** offers many facts about the kind of the beasts:*
- *A lion sleeps up to 20 hours daily.*
- *An average lion life span is 15 to 20 years.*
- *At five months, lion cubs weigh up to 50 pounds.*
- *An adult male can weigh from 450 to 500 pounds.*
- *The lioness does the actual hunting for the group.*
- *Litters usually include one to five cubs.*

ANIMALS & THE GREAT OUTDOORS

The casino hotels are home to several animal displays featuring some of their performers. **The Tiger Habitat at The Mirage**, *Tel. 702/791-7111,* showcases the beautiful white tigers of the Siegfried and Roy show. The animals can be seen anytime; admission is free.

Also at the Mirage, the **Dolphin Habitat** is home to six dolphins. You can watch the playful mammals from above or go below the water level for a closer view. There are tours of the habitat conducted from 11am-7pm weekdays and 9am-7pm on weekends. Admission is $3; free for kids 10 and under if accompanied by an adult.

Just down the street, the **Lion Habitat at the MGM Grand**, *3799 Las Vegas Boulevard South, Tel. 702/891-7777, www.mgmgrand.com,* features the symbols of MGM. This $9 million feature is new to the hotel and is located near the entertainment dome. In this unique attraction, you can walk through a clear tunnel with lions both above and below you. The habitat consists of waterfalls, a pond, Acacia trees, and stones. On any day, you'll

LIBERACE SCHOLARSHIPS

You might think of Liberace as only the glittery showman, but the Liberace Foundation for the Performing Arts regularly awards scholarships. Since 1976, the foundation has awarded over $4 million in scholarships for the arts to over 100 institutions.

"We have Liberace Scholars this year in music, dance, drama, film and the visual arts," said Sandra L. Harris, Executive Director of The Liberace Museum, which funds The Liberace Foundation. "We are very pleased with the diversity of the scholarships being awarded. It is with great pleasure that we continue The Foundation's mission of helping talented people in the arts study their craft and pursue their dreams."

see anywhere from one to five lions in the habitat (but the lions do take breaks through day). Admission is free.

For something more natural, head to the **UNLV Arboretum**, *University of Nevada, 4505 S. Maryland Parkway, Tel. 702/895-3392.* This garden has over 40 types of trees and is open for self-guided tours.

Sometimes it might seem like the only stellar lights visible in Las Vegas are of the neon variety, but you will have the chance to see stars of a more natural variety at the **Planetarium** at the *Community College of Southern Nevada, 3200 E. Cheyenne Ave., Tel. 651-4759.* The planetarium has shows at 6pm and 7:30 pm on Fridays and 3:30pm and 7:30pm on Saturdays. After the last showing, there are public viewing sessions at the observatory, the only public planetarium and observatory in Southern Nevada. Admission is $4 for adults, $3 for children.

It's not the San Diego Zoo, but you will find a collection of animals at the **Southern Nevada Zoological-Botanical Park**, *1775 N. Rancho Drive, Tel. 702/647-4685, www.lvrj.com/communitylink/zoo.* The park's goal is to highlight endangered species and habitat protection, and children will be able to view endangered cats, the last family of Barbary Apes in the country, as well as species such as wallabies, chimps, eagles, emus, and more.

Of special local interest, the park contains every venomous reptile species that's native to Southern Nevada. If you're interested in local history and ecology, check out the tours offered by the zoological foundation in Chapter 2. Admission to the zoo is $5.95 for adults, $3.95 for kids 2-12 and free for children under 2 years of age. The park is open daily from 9-4:30pm.

Bird lovers in the family will also be interested in the **Gilcrease Bird Sanctuary**, *8101 Racel Road, Tel. 702/645-4224 or 658-6014.* This sanctuary is home to many injured birds that are being rehabilitated. Look for game birds, birds of prey and also colorful exotics. The sanctuary is open Wednesday-Sunday from 10am-4pm; admission is $3 for adults and $1 for children.

Bird lovers should also make a stop at the **Flamingo Hilton**, *3555 Las Vegas Boulevard South, Tel. 702/733-3111 or 800/732-2111,* to have a look at the flamingo habitat, filled with Chilean flamingos as well as African penguins, swans, ducks, turtles, and more.

MUSEUMS & EXHIBITS

Museums in Vegas range from terrific to tacky...but they can all be fun. Some have been added to casinos as yet another way to lure you into their gaming areas, but even these are done with good taste and a bulging budget.

One of the best museums for families in town is the **Lied Discovery Children's Museum**, *833 Las Vegas Boulevard North, Tel. 702/382-3445.* Kids enjoy this museum for its many hands-on displays and exhibits and are encouraged to take part in the many displays to learn more about science, the arts, and the world around them. The museum is open 10am-5pm Tuesday-Sunday. Admission is $5 for adults, $4 for children 2-17, and free for children 1 year and younger.

Our favorite museum in town is **The Tomb and Museum of King Tutankhamen**, *The Luxor, 3900 Las Vegas Boulevard South, Tel. 702/262-4555.* We've visited the real thing and, while it's not quite the same, the weather's a lot cooler at this version and the flight's a lot easier. Unlike the real tomb, at this full-scale version you'll see the tomb just as it looked when it was discovered by archaeologist Howard Carter in 1922, complete with the tomb riches, linens, tools, and, of course, the famous sarcophagus. You'll take a self-guided audio tour through the tomb. The museum is open 9am-11pm daily (and until 1am on Friday and Saturday nights); admission is $5.

One of the most unique museum displays in town is **"Titanic: The Exhibition,"** on an unlimited display at the *Rio Suites Hotel and Casino, www.playrio.com/titanic/index.htm*. This exhibit is presented by RMS Titanic, the company that has salvage rights to the 1912 shipwreck, and it's filled with over 200 items. Along with multimedia displays, the exhibit includes the D Deck portal where first-class passengers walked aboard that fateful cruise. The giant door has never before been exhibited. While we think younger children would be bored by the exhibit, pre-teens and teens who were fans of the movie will really appreciate the displays. (Note: You won't be able to take your cameras or videorecorders into this exhibit.) Tickets for the exhibit are on sale at the Titanic Box Office which is on the second floor of the Masquerade Village; you can also call Ticketmaster, *Tel. 702/474-4000*, to reserve your tickets. The exhibit is open from 10am-10pm daily.

Starstruck in Vegas but haven't seen any familiar faces? You're guaranteed some stellar sightings at **Madame Tussaud's Celebrity Encounter**, *The Venetian, 3355 Las Vegas Boulevard South, Tel. 702/367-1847, www.madame-tussauds.com*. This sprawling museum has wax figures of celebrities ranging from Whoopi Goldberg to Elton John (plus plenty of other older stars the kids won't recognize). The museum is divided into five theme areas. Kids will like "The Big Night," which features Whoopi Goldberg, Brad Pitt, Jerry Springer, Oprah and other present-day faces. Sports buffs will spot some familiar faces in "The Big Night," where figures of Babe Ruth, Joe Montana and others stand.

Tickets for the museum are $12.50 (there's a discount if you're a Nevada resident), $10 for kids 4-12, and free for kids three and under. The museum is open daily 10am-10pm. In "Madame Tussaud's Story," the process of making wax figures is explained. "Rock and Pop" displays popular rock icons such as Elton John an Bruce Springsteen. "Las Vegas Legends" will probably be lost on the younger kids; it features the names synonymous with Vegas: Frank Sinatra, Tony Bennett, Tom Jones, and others. The final section is "Finale," and pays tribute to the glittery city with fun animatronic figures kids will enjoy.

HEARING VOICES?

You might not just see celebrities in Las Vegas, you very well may hear them as well. If you take the audio tour of the Treasures of Mandalay Bay Museum, you'll hear the voice of John O'Hurley, the actor who played Seinfeld's J. Peterman. Call the MGM Grand Hotel, and the phone will be answered by the voice of Tommy Tune. Take the Star Trek: The Experience tour and you'll hear Patrick Stewart in his role as Captain Jean-Luc Picard. Stroll the Secret Garden at the Mirage and you'll hear Siegfried and Roy, and when you head through McCarran Airport, you'll be told to hold the handrail and stay to the right by celebs like Rich Little, Gladys Knight, Bobby Vinton, Judy Tenuta, Wolfgang Puck and others.

Only in Las Vegas would you find this unique museum: **Elvis-A-Rama**, *Industrial Rd. west of the Strip, Tel. 702/309-7200.* It may sound hokey, but this museum packs in $3 million worth of Elvis memorabilia, from a purple Cadillac the King owned to a gold lamé suit to movie clothes he wore in his films. There's a 50's style cafe here and the museum is visited by an Elvis impersonator several times a day, performing on a small stage. Cost is $9.95 for adults; kids 12 and under are free. The museum is open 10-7 daily.

Certainly a symbol of Las Vegas's glitz and glamour is the late Liberace, remembered at the **Liberace Museum**, *1775 East Tropicana Avenue, Tel. 702/798-5595, www.liberace.org.* This museum isn't going to attract just any kid, but those with an interest in pianos and valuable cars might enjoy a visit. Eighteen of the performer's pianos are on display (including a rhinestone-covered piano), as well as cars, costumes (yes, even a black diamond mink lined with over 40,000 rhinestones), and more. Kids enjoy the miniature piano collection (don't miss the one made of 10,000 toothpicks!)

To be honest, we didn't think we'd enjoy the museum when we visited, but found it well done and with exhibits that really are fun to view, even if you didn't have an idea who Liberace was. The museum is open daily from 10am to 5pm and Sunday from 1pm to 5pm. Admission donations are $6.95 for adults, $4.95 for seniors and students, and kids under 12 are free when accompanied by an adult.

Kids love the **Guinness World of Records Museum**, *2780 Las Vegas Boulevard South, Tel. 702/792-3766, www.guinnessmuseum.com.* It's all here – tacky to terrific in life-size replica. The museum is open daily 9am-8pm; admission is $4.95 for adults, $295 for kids ages 5-12. children under 5 are admitted free.

One of Las Vegas's most unique museums is the **World of Coca Cola**, *at Showcase Mall, 3785 Las Vegas Boulevard South, Tel. 800/720-COKE.* Yes, this is home to the world's tallest Coke bottle over 100 feet tall. You'll ride the bottle's elevators to the museum that takes you back on a sentimental journey through the world of Coke. Admission is $3.50 for adults (kids three and under are admitted free); the museum is open daily from 10am-8pm.

Liberace was quite the car buff. In building one of the **Liberace Museum**, *1775 East Tropicana Avenue, 702/798-5595,* *www.liberace.org*, you'll find an entire car gallery. Highlights include a 1934 Mercedes Excalibur (covered in Austrian Rhinestones, of course), a 1954 custom red, white, and blue Rolls Royce, a Phantom V Landau Mirrored Rolls Royce Limousine (one of only seven made), and even a pink Volks-Royce, used at Radio City Music Hall to drive the fur cape with 16-foot train off the stage. The museum is open daily from 10am to 5pm and Sunday from 1pm to 5pm. Admission donations are $6.95 for adults, $4.95 for seniors and students, and kids under 12 are free when accompanied by an adult.

The **Imperial Palace Auto Collection**, *Imperial Palace, Tel. 800/ 634-3441*, was the first car museum we ever visited and we were prepared not to like it. Surprisingly, though, even for non-car buffs, this is a fun stop. The collection has over 200 cars ranging from antiques to one-of-a-kind vehicles. Admission is $6.95 for adults and $3 for kids 12 and under; the collection is open 9:30am-11:30pm daily.

Learn more about the natural world around Las Vegas at the **UNLV Barrick Museum of Natural History**, *University of Nevada, Las Vegas, 4505 South Maryland Parkway, Tel. 702/ 895-3381*. The museum is open weekdays 8am-4:45 and Saturdays 10-2. Admission is free.

There are more natural history exhibits found at the **Las Vegas Natural History Museum**, *900 Las Vegas Boulevard North, Tel. 702/ 384-3466*. This museum has exhibits that trace the area's residents from the days of the dinosaurs. Especially fun for kids are the live sharks on display and the interactive displays. Admission is $5.50, $4.50 for students, $3 for kids 4-12, and under 3 are free.

Are you and your kids interested in history? There is a history to Las Vegas that predates the oldest slot machines in town. **Lost**

City Museum of Archaeology, *Overton, 60 miles north of Las Vegas, Tel. 702/397-2193.* We enjoyed this museum and recommend it, even though it is a drive from the city. It contains an extensive collection of Pueblo Indian artifacts and even a reconstruction of an Indian pueblo. Admission is $2; the museum is open 8:30-4:30 daily.

Another historic site is the **Old Las Vegas Mormon Fort State Historic Park**, *500 East Washington, Tel. 702/486-3511.* This historic site is just a mile from downtown but it transports visitors back to the days of the mid-19th century. Call for hours.

FACTORY TOURS

Until recently, Las Vegas and nearby Henderson had several good factory tours of interest to kids (well, at least the free sweets samples at the end of the tour were of interest to kids). Today, the factory tours have dwindled but we think kids will still be interested in **Ron Lee's World of Clowns**, *380 Carousel Parkway, Henderson, Tel. 702/434-1700.* This tour explains how clowns as well as animated sculptures are created. To reach this site, which is about 10 miles from the Strip, take Tropicana to Eastern, turn left at Sunset, right on Gibson, then right on Warm Springs to Carousel Parkway. Admission is free; the facility is open 8-5 weekdays, 9-5 weekends.

Another good family choice is the **Ethel M Chocolates Tour**, *2 Cactus Garden Drive, Henderson, Tel. 702/433-2500.* In Las Vegas, there are few sure things. In this land of glitter and gold, the big winners are the casinos and the vacationers who come with the plan of just having a good time.

But the Ethel M Chocolate Factory and Cactus Gardens are winning bets. The admission is free, the gardens are both beautiful and educational, the factory tour is interesting, and you'll hit the jackpot with a free sample of the world famous chocolate.

Lady Luck couldn't tempt you with better odds.

The Ethel M Chocolate Factory was founded in 1978, but its history dates back much earlier. The company is named for Ethel Mars, whose son, Forrest Mars, began (you guessed it) Mars bars. It's a family tree firmly rooted in chocolate, counting among their creations Milky Way, Three Musketeers, Snickers, and M & M candies.

Unlike the mass-produced chocolates of the family line, the Ethel M product is the result of a much smaller operation. Using machinery imported from Italy, the chocolates are created in "batch" or small quantities. Over 50 varieties are prepared in the 100,000-square-foot factory. You can observe the intricate candy-making process on self-guided tours daily.

Your vantage point is a glassed hallway overlooking the production area. Video monitors overhead explain the processes performed throughout the factory to over 1,800 guests a day. The production of these high-quality chocolates takes place in two areas: kitchen preparation and production. First, factory associates prepare the candy centers. Fillings range from butter creams to caramels.

Next, the chocolates are "enrobed" or coasted with either milk or dark chocolate. A curtain of chocolate flows over the candy pieces to achieve an even coat. Now the candy heads to the holding machine, which shakes to ensure that no air bubbles are trapped in the chocolate.

The pieces are then cooled and the cordials and liqueur creams are filled. A bottom chocolate shell is added and the candy is complete.

From here, the candies are hand-packed. The shelf life of some varieties is as short as two weeks, so shipments are made quickly from the factory.

After your self-guided tour, you'll wind up in the **Ethel M Chocolate Shoppe**, where your free sample awaits. You can choose from any of the factory products: butter creams, nuts, toffees, coins, truffles, fudge, or their most famous creation: liqueur creams. Available only to those over 21, the chocolates are filled with liqueurs ranging from amaretto to creme de menthe to Irish creme. (Kids will find free, non-alcoholic samples.)

But at the factory, dessert is only half the fun. Outside the doors lies desert – a beautiful 2.5 acre **cactus garden** featuring local and exotic varieties to help you appreciate the Nevada landscape.

Over 350 varieties of cacti and succulents are represented in these gardens. You'll find numerous species, such as ocotillo, paloverde trees, beaver tail, purple pancake, missionary cactus, cholla cactus, Chilean mesquite trees, Texas sage, and agave or century plants. Many other plants were imported from Argentina and Mexico and neighboring Arizona, home of the giant saguaros. Most plants are identified with both common and scientific names, as well as their place of origin.

This garden displays the rugged characteristics required of desert plants, but most of all, it is a place to enjoy the splendor of the desert. During April and May, the plants display breathtaking blossoms as colorful as those found in any rose garden.

To create the cactus gardens, the Ethel M brought in over 400 tons of rock, including Arizona moss rock and, appropriately enough, Bali Hai "chocolate" rock from Utah. The rock provides a rugged background for the cacti and succulents.

These gardens provide visitors an excellent opportunity to see some native flora, a sight not often seen along the neon-studded Strip. Here you'll have a chance to view the prickly plants that are well-suited to this dry climate where summer afternoons often top 100 degrees, and where temperatures as high as 117 have been recorded.

The factory and gardens are located fifteen minutes from the Strip on the way to Hoover Dam. Drive east on Tropicana to Mountain Vista (5.5 miles), then turn right on Mountain Vista. Continue two miles to Sunset Way. Turn left at the traffic light into Green Valley Business Park, then turn left on Cactus Garden Drive.

7. CAN I PLAY OUTSIDE?

PARKS, PLAYGROUNDS, & SPORTS FUN

Las Vegas may seem like a world of concrete and neon but there's a natural side beyond the glitter. Parks, sporting areas, and plenty of places to play and picnic await families.

PARKS

If you're like most people, you probably picture Las Vegas as a world of concrete and casinos, not ballfields and picnic grounds. Well, Las Vegas is home to plenty of residents who look for weekend fun with their kids, and there are numerous parks in the area that you can enjoy as well. Here's a listing of several parks where you'll find a break from the hustle and bustle of the Strip and chance for a quiet picnic:

Alexander Villas Park, *3620 Lincoln Road*: This park has a picnic area as well as basketball courts and other facilities.

Davis Park, *2796 Redwood St.*: This park includes picnic grounds as well as a playground.

Desert Bloom Park, *8405 S. Maryland Parkway*: look for picnic grounds as well as playgrounds, basketball courts, and more here.

Desert Breeze Park, *8425 Spring Mountain Road*: You'll find playgrounds as well as skateboarding area and basketball courts here.

Grapevine Springs Park, *5480 Palm*: This park includes picnic areas and playgrounds.

Hidden Palms Park, *8855 Hidden Palms Pkwy.*: Look for picnic grounds as well as a playground, tennis courts, and basketball courts here.

Horseman's Park, *5800 E. Flamingo Rd.*: This park includes picnic grounds.

Laurelwood Park, *4300 Newcastle Rd.*: Picnic areas as well as playgrounds, tennis courts, and basketball fields are available here.

Lewis Family Park, *1970 Tree Line Drive*: This extensive park has picnic grounds, playgrounds, horseshoe pits, tennis courts, and more.

Lone Mountain Park, *4445 N. Jensen*: Picnic, let the kids enjoy the playground or skateboard and rollerblade in a specially designated area.

Magdalena's Vegas Mountain Park, *4580 Vegas Valley Drive*: This park offers a picnic area.

Maslow Park, *4902 Lana Drive*: Picnic grounds, playgrounds, a swimming pool, and more are offered here.

Paul Meyer Park, *4525 New Forest Drive*: This park includes picnicking, playgrounds, tennis, and more.

Nellis Meadows Park, *4949 E. Cheyenne Avenue*: This park offers picnicking, playgrounds, and ball fields.

Paradise Park, *4770 S. Harrison Drive*: This park includes picnic areas, horseshoe pits, tennis, volleyball, basketball, and more.

Paradise Vista Park, *5582 Stirrup Street*: Picnicking, horseshoe pits, and playgrounds are found here.

Parkdale Park, *3200 Ferndale Street*: Here you'll find picnicking, playgrounds, a swimming pool, basketball courts, and more.

Prosperity Park, *7101 Parasol Lane*: Look for picnic grounds, playgrounds, and basketball courts here.

Shadow Rock Park, *2650 Los Feliz*: Picnicking, playgrounds, and ballfields here.

Silver Bowl Sports Complex, *6800 E. Russell Road*: This extensive park includes picnic grounds, playgrounds, and special features like radio controlled air field and car track.

Sunrise Park, *2240 Linn Lane*: Look for picnic grounds, playgrounds, swimming pool, basketball courts, and more here.

Sunset Park and Lake, *2601 E. Sunset Road*: This extensive park has picnicking, playgrounds, swimming pool, tennis, basketball courts, horseshoe pits, a course for disc golf, radio controlled boating, and more.

Whitney Park, *5700 Missouri*: Look for a swimming pool, picnicking, playgrounds, tennis, and more here.

For more on area parks, contact the **Clark County Department of Parks and Recreation**, *Tel. 702/4558200 or www.co.clark.nv.us/ PARKREC/urban.htm.*

SUMMER HEAT

In Las Vegas you'll find the mercury regularly rising to the three-digit level on summer days. In these conditions, you'll need to take extra precautions to make sure the kids – and you – don't fall ill.

The first concern is heat cramps, muscle cramps caused because of lost water and salt in the body. From there, it's not far to heat exhaustion, when the body tries to cool itself off and the victim feels, well, exhausted and even nauseous. Finally, heat stroke can set in, a life-threatening condition.

What can you do to avoid these conditions?

• First, drink water – lots of water. Everyone should drink plenty of water and don't wait until you're thirsty to reach for the water jug. Thirst is an early sign of heat stress so start drinking before it reaches that point.

• Slow down. Curtail your activities whenever possible and do like the animals do in the high heat – move slowly.

• Take lots of breaks.

• Stay out of the direct sun.

• Make sure everyone is protected from the sun. Put wide brimmed hats and caps on the kids as well as sunglasses.

• Wear sunscreen. Sunburned skin is a definite no-no.

• Avoid the hours between 10am and 2pm, that's when the sun's rays are the strongest. Enjoy an early morning hike then kick back and take a swim break that afternoon.

SPORTS & RECREATION
BOATING

Near Las Vegas, you'll find several options for boating. Houseboating is the most popular option with families, who will find that lazy days spent on the water will long bring back many vacation memories.

Forever Resorts, *Callville Bay Marina-Lake Mead, Tel. 702/565-4813*, has houseboats for rent. Seven Crown Resorts Houseboat Getaways, *Tel. 800/752-9669*, also has houseboats available for rent.

Want someone else to take the wheel? You'll find guided cruises on Lake Mead available through **Lake Mead Cruises**, *Boulder City, Tel. 702/293-6180*. Along with cruises, the company offers tours of Hoover Dam.

RAFTING

We'll never forget our experience on **Black Canyon River Raft Tours**, *1297 Nevada Hwy., Boulder, Tel. 702/293-3776 or 800/696-RAFT, www.rafts.com*. We put in the water just below Hoover Dam on a hot, hot August day for a memorable half day river journey. The ride was a wonderful float down the Colorado, with a stop for a picnic lunch along the way. We floated through spectacular canyons in remote regions that were hard to imagine as just a short drive from the city.

You'll find, however, that the water below Hoover Dam is, because of the depth of the lake, extremely cold. As hard to believe as it is, carry along a windbreaker jacket for this raft trip, even on days like the one we experienced with 110 degree temperatures in the canyon and bone chilling water in the river.

BOWLING

If your family loves to bowl, you're in luck. Las Vegas is home to many good bowling facilities, some of tournament class. The biggest and best is the **Showboat Hotel and Casino**, *2800 Fremont Street, Tel. 702/385-9153*. We stayed here once during a bowling tournament and the talk was bowling, bowling, bowling around the clock. Even if you're not a tournament class player, you'll enjoy the excellent facilities that are open 24 hours daily. The bowling center has 106 lanes.

Several other casino hotels offer good facilities as well. **Gold Coast Hotel and Casino**, *4000 W. Flamingo Road, Tel. 702/367-4700*, has 72 bowling lanes and is open 24 hours daily. **Orleans Hotel and Casino**, *4500 W. Tropicana, Tel. 702/365-7111*, is also open around the clock and offers 70 lanes. **Sam's Town**, *5111 Boulder Highway, Tel. 702/456-7777 or 800/634-6371, Fax 702/454-8014, www.samstownlv.com*, also offers on-site bowling.

Santa Fe Bowling Center, *4949 N. Rancho Drive, Tel. 702/658-4995*, is open 24 hours and has 60 lanes.

CAMPING

It's not just anywhere that you can pull in your RV and camp right next to the world's biggest circus. At **Circusland Recreational Vehicle Park**, *Circus-Circus, 800/444-2472 or 702/734-0410*, families with RVs find 399 spaces with full hookups. The park is just steps from the hotel and the theme park but there are plenty of attractive features right on site: a pool, playground, game arcade, pool table, Laundromat, and a general store.

HORSEBACK RIDING

Your family can saddle up at the **Red Rock Riding Stables**, *Red Rock Canyon, Tel. 702/387-2457 or 702/566-7160, www.cowboytrailrides.com*. The stables offer several different programs from which to choose including hourly rides (the best choice for new riders), half-day, full-day and overnight rides.

INDOOR SKYDIVING

Flyaway Indoor Skydiving, *200 Convention Center Drive, Tel. 702/731-4768 or 877/545-8093.* This is a unique ride – it gives you the feeling of skydiving but in the safety of an indoor facility. The riders put on special flight suits and float in a wind tunnel, hovering over winds up to 120 mph. You start with a 15-minute training class then you and up to four more flyers enjoy a 15-minute ride. The cost is $35 for the first flight (you can also buy a book of five flights for $100, all for the same rider).

Restrictions: Riders must weigh at least 40 pounds but no more than 230 pounds. You need to wear socks and soft soled shoes.

ROCK CLIMBING

Kids got you climbing the walls? Put that energy to good use with an indoor rock climb. Kids and adults enjoy this (well, we think the kids like it more than most out-of-shape adults). This makes a good rainy day or it's-so-hot-we've-got-to-stay-inside day activity.

You'll find indoor climbing walls at several parks in town:

All-American SportPark, *121 E. Sunset Road, Tel. 702/317-7777, www.sportparkvegas.com.* The park is open 11am-11pm (until midnight Friday and Saturday nights). An unlimited attraction pass is available for $14.95.

Powerhouse Indoor Climbing Center, *8201 W. Charleston Boulevard, Tel. 702/254-5604.* Day passes are $12 here and include use of all the many terrains they've got available here, enough to satisfy even the toughest mountain goat in the family.

When you hear Gameworks, you may think of arcade games, but his entertainment center has a lot more. **Gameworks**, *Showcase Mall, 3785 Las Vegas Boulevard South, Tel. 702/ 432-4263*, is home to the Sega Power Sled with three sleds that riders steer (yes, even in a town that doesn't see snow); you'll also find what's called the world's tallest free-standing rock-climbing structure here. When you get hungry, there's a restaurant and some snack bars here. Gameworks is open 10 am to 4 am daily.

SNOW SKIING

Snow skiing in Las Vegas? Yep, right outside town you'll find snow skiing from Thanksgiving to Easter. **Las Vegas Ski and Snowboard Resort at Lee Canyon**, *Tel. 702/ 593-9500*, can set you up with equipment, lessons, whatever you need.

ICE SKATING

Santa Fe Ice Arena, *Santa Fe, 4949 N. Rancho Drive, Tel. 702/ 658-4991*, is a huge facility. Kids can rent skates here for $2 for hockey skates, $1.50 for figure skates; admission is $5 or $4 for kids 12 and under.

The **Sahara Ice Palace**, *800 Karen Ave., Tel. 702/260-7465*, has public skating Monday through Friday from 3-5pm, 8-10pm Friday and Saturday, and 1-4 on weekends. Skates rent for $2 and admission is $5 for adults, $4 for kids under 12.

ROLLER SKATING

All-American SportPark, *121 E. Sunset Road, Tel. 702/317-7777*, has roller skating.

PROFESSIONAL SPORTS

The **Las Vegas Stars** baseball team, *Tel. 702/798-7825, E-mail: lvstarstixs@aol.com, www.lasvegasstars.com*, is a minor league farm team for the San Diego Padres. The team plays at Cashman Field.

Tickets can be obtained through Ticketmaster, *Tel. 702/474-4000* or *www.ticketmaster.com.*

RODEO

Las Vegas is the home of the **National Rodeo Finals**, *Tel. 702/895-3900,* every December. This mega-event stretches on for two weeks at the Thomas and Mack Center but you'll need advance tickets for this very popular event.

SPORTS PARKS

Several sports parks in town offer hours of activities:

All-American Sportspark, *121 E. Sunset Road, Tel. 702/317-7777, www.sportparkvegas.com,* has all types of activities for energetic families including batting cages, roller skating, an indoor rock climbing facility, an arcade, NASCAR speedway, and more. The highlights include the NASCAR speedpark; go carters find three tracks here. The MLB Slugger Stadium has 16 batting stations while Rockreation offers indoor climbing wall. The park is open 11am-11pm Monday to Thursday, 11am-midnight Friday-Saturday, 11am-10pm Sunday.

Restrictions: there are height restrictions on some rides.

All-American Sportspark/Callaway Golf Center, *6730 Las Vegas Boulevard South, Tel. 702/896-4100.* Like its sister facility above, this park has NASCAR tracks for go-cart races, batting cages, and more; this park also has a golf center with a driving range.

Scandia Family Fun Center, *2900 Sirius Ave., Tel. 702/364-0070.* This park has go-cart racing, pitching machines, bumper boats, and three miniature golf courses. The park is open 10am-

10pm daily. You'll pay for each activity you play but you can also buy an all-day pass.

LASER TAG

Get ready to enter a maze lit with black lights and filled with fog at **Laser Quest**, *7361 W. Lake Mead Boulevard, Tel. 702/243-8881.* Players enter the maze for a 20-minute game. Games are offered from 2pm to 10 pm Tuesday through Thursday or 2pm to midnight Friday, noon to midnight Saturday, and noon to 8 pm Sunday.

At **Adventure Dome at Circus Circus**, *2880 Las Vegas Boulevard South, 794-3939, www.adventuredome.com,* you can enjoy laser tag as well as a whole host of other rides. At the park's **Lazer Blast Laser Tag**, players don special jackets for a five-minute game. The cost for an unlimited ride pass is $12.95 for kids 33 to 47 inches tall and $16.95 for travelers over 48 inches high. Kids under 33 inches tall come in for free. The hours vary by season so check with the hotel before making your plans.

Restriction: game participants must be 42 inches tall.

At **Coney Island Emporium**, *New York-New York Hotel & Casino, 3790 Las Vegas Boulevard S., Tel. 702/740-6969,* has interactive laser tag as well as many other games. Restriction: Children under the age of 18, unaccompanied by a parent, legal guardian or responsible adult over the age of 21, are prohibited from the arcade during these hours: Sunday - Thursday, after 10 p.m.; Friday, Saturday & Nevada School Holidays, after 12 midnight; and Memorial Day - Labor Day, after 12 midnight.

PAINTBALL

Looking for paintball fun? There are several options in town. If you've got a serious paintball fan at home, consider a call before you leave home. Several operators offer a discount if participants come with their own paintball gun.

Desert Storm Paintball Games, *North Jones Boulevard, one mile beyond the asphalt, Tel. 702/595-2555,* offers paintball fun in a supervised environment. Games are scheduled and you can also reserve a play time, so be sure to call ahead.

Restriction: players must to at least 10 years old to participate; also, players must bring their own equipment.

Vegas Indoor Paintball Area (VIPA), *2760 South Highland Drive, Tel. 702/893-8472,* is a 12,000-square-foot facility and is open from 6pm - midnight Friday and Saturday nights. Cost is $20 for rental.

8. WHAT CAN I BUY?

Any money travelers might have won at the tables is the target of the many shops found just steps from the casinos. Every casino hotel has an arcade of beautiful shops offered in one last attempt to keep those winnings in house. Several of the shopping areas have features of special interest to families. Las Vegas is also home to some traditional shopping malls as well.

SHOPPING CENTERS

The **Fashion Show Mall**, *3200 Las Vegas Boulevard South, Tel. 702/369-8382,* is a landmark on the Strip thanks to its location across from Treasure Island. You'll find plenty of high end stores like Saks Fifth Avenue and Macy's here as well as family-friendly features like a food court. Open weekdays 10am-9pm, Saturday 10am-7pm, and Sunday 10am-6pm.

The **Forum Shops at Caesars**, *3500 Las Vegas Boulevard South, Tel. 702/893-4800,* may be a mall, but it's unlike any other mall you've ever seen. The mall boasts ritzy names you'd expect to see here including Versace and Benini, but also kid favorites like FAO Schwarz. Of special interest, the mall is home to many special features.

Another large casino shopping center is **The Tower Shops at Stratosphere Hotel and Casino**, *2000 Las Vegas Boulevard South, Tel. 702/383-4790.* This mall is decorated with street scenes from cities like New York, Paris and Hong Kong.

The biggest mall in town (actually in Nevada) is **The Boulevard Mall**, *3528 Maryland Parkway, Tel. 702/735-8268.* The mall is just a few minutes from the major tourist areas.

Another large mall is **Meadows Mall**, *4300 Meadows Lane (at US95 and Valley View Boulevard), Tel. 702/702/878-4849.* This mall is two-story and has over 140 stores. Open 10am-9pm weekdays, 10-5 weekends.

FACTORY OUTLETS

In search of a bargain? You've got a few options:

Belz Factory Outlet World, *7400 Las Vegas Boulevard South, Tel. 702/896-5599,* is home to almost 150 stores as well as two food courts where even the pickiest eater will find something good.

Factory Stores of America, *9155 Las Vegas Boulevard South, Tel. 702/897-9090,* has over 50 stores.

9. WHO'S GOING TO TAKE CARE OF ME?

Remember, we said that this book is Las Vegas *with* Kids, not Las Vegas *for* Kids. You'll need to plan most activities with the kids as supervised options for young travelers are somewhat limited. If you do want to sneak off for a couple of hours of gambling, you have two options for young children: supervised programs and babysitters.

HOTEL SUPERVISED PROGRAMS

One of the best supervised programs in town is the **MGM Grand Youth Activity Center**, *MGM Grand, 3799 Las Vegas Boulevard South, Tel. 702/891-1111 or 800/929-1111, www.mgmgrand.com.* This is the only supervised program on the Strip and it's open to guests and non-guests alike. The center accepts young visitors between the ages of 3 and 12. Most of the activities are in-house and involve air hockey, Nintendo, movies, arts and crafts, table tennis, and board games. Kids are served meals and on certain days children are taken to the theme park.

The Orleans, *4500 West Tropicana, Tel. 702/365-7111, www.orleanscasino.com,* offers a kids' program for ages 3 months to 12 years fro 9 am to midnight daily. There's a maximum stay of 3 1/2 hours.

Gold Coast, *4000 West Flamingo Road, Tel. 702/367-7111, www.goldcoastcasino.com,* offers free day care for the children of guests. Participants in the program must be between three and eight years old and must be potty trained. You can leave the kids here for no more than three hours between the hours of 9am and midnight daily.

Boulder Station, *4111 Boulder Highway, Tel. 702/432-7777,* offers a supervised program called Kids Quest for children six months to 12 years of age. Kids can stay no more than 5 hours. If your child is under age 2, you'll need to make reservations. The program includes free video games, movies, and games for all ages. The charge varies by the age of your child and the day of the week.

Texas Station, *2101 Texas Star Ln. North, Tel. 702/631-1000, www.texasstation.com,* also offers Kids Quest with the same rules as Boulder Station.

BABYSITTING

In-room babysitting is also available. Costs will vary depending on the hour, the age of children, and the service, but expect to pay from $25-$50 for the first four hours, and anywhere from $5-9 for each additional hour. Expect to pay more for late night appointments and on holidays.

The best way to find a reliable in-room sitter is to talk with your hotel's concierge. Ask for their recommendations.

Next, get in touch with the babysitting services. Ask specific questions: are the baby-sitters trained in CPR? Have background checks been run on all employees? Reliable services should be happy to answer these questions and to provide documentation.

Below find a list of a few of Las Vegas's in-room babysitting services. We don't endorse these companies but offer them as a service for you to check out:

Four Season's Baby-sitting Service
Tel. 702/384-5848

Grandma Dotti's Baby-sitting
Tel. 702/456-1175

Nanny's & Granny's
Tel. 702/364-4700

Precious Commodities
Tel. 702/871-1191

10. DO I HAVE TO GO TO BED?

NIGHTLIFE - WITH KIDS - IN LAS VEGAS

Las Vegas is definitely a city that comes out after dark, perhaps more than any other destination on earth. You'll see a whole other side to the city after the sun sets, one that's lit by the glow of neon and filled with excitement.

Much of that excitement is aimed at adults. Adult shows – many topless – are a Las Vegas standard, but you will find shows that welcome families.

You'll also find other after-dark activities, from the one-of-a-kind Fremont Street Experience to movie theaters.

FAMILY APPROPRIATE SHOWS

Siegfried and Roy, *The Mirage, 3500 Las Vegas Boulevard South, Tel. 702/792-7777*, is a Vegas favorite, a lavish extravaganza. We enjoyed the enormous magic feats that involve white tigers and lions; you've got to see these tricks to believe them – and even then you won't understand how on earth they did that! The show is pricey at $95 but the run of this one is limited. The Siegfried and

GETTING SHOW RESERVATIONS

Call the showroom for show tickets. You'll want to have a credit card ready for advance reservations. Some shows only sell tickets on the day of the show, and some shows require you to buy tickets in person at the box office. You can also visit the ticket desk at your hotel for tickets to shows at other hotels.

Roy contract expires at the end of 2001 and they haven't yet renewed at press time. Shows are presented at 7:30pm and 11pm, Friday through Tuesday. Admission price includes the show, tax, gratuity, two drinks, and a souvenir program.

Ready for some star sightings? Well at **Legends in Concert**, *Imperial Palace, 3535 Las Vegas Boulevard South, Tel. 702/794-3261,* you won't be seeing the real things, but you will see some mighty good impressions. Kids might recognize some names impersonated here like Elton John but the bits featuring Roy Orbison, Sammy Davis Jr., and Liberace will probably be lost on them. Shows are held at 7:30pm and 10:30pm Monday through Saturday; price is $34.50 for adults, $19.50 for kids 12 and under.

For a real one-of-a-kind show, don't miss **Cirque du Soleil's Mystère**, *Treasure Island, 3300 Las Vegas Boulevard South, Tel. 702/894-7111 or 800/944-7444, Fax 702/894-7446, www.treasureisland.com.* This troupe of 72 entertainers includes gymnasts, clows, musicians and acrobats from numerous countries. This show has often been named the best in Las Vegas and it is one that is truly unique. Ticket prices are $75.00 and can be purchased at the Cirque du Soleil ticket offices at Treasure Island and The Mirage. Shows are held Wednesday through Sunday. You can also reserve tickets up to three months before the show date; call *800/392-1999* or *702/796-9999.*

The magic show of **Lance Burton**, *Monte Carlo Resort and Casino, 3770 Las Vegas Boulevard South, Tel. 702/730-7777 or 800/311-8999, Fax 702/730-7200, www.monte-carlo.com,* is a favorite with families. This is another one of those shows you'll have to see to believe (and even then you'll still be left wondering how on earth he performed those sleight of hand tricks). Burton's act incorporates white doves, ducks, and plenty of fun and the master magician often brings children from the audience up on the stage. The show is performed twice a day at 7pm and 10pm (shoot for the 7pm if you can); the cost is $49.95 for the main floor, $44.95 for balcony seats.

Looking for more of a bargain show? Then check out **"The Voice of Magic with Darren Romeo"** at the Flamingo Hilton, *3555 Las Vegas Boulevard South, Tel. 702/733-3111 or 800/732-2111, Fax 702/733-3353, www.lv-flamingo.com.* This show is the town's best bargain at just $14.95 and includes magic performed with a full menu of show tunes. The shows are scheduled for afternoons, another plus for traveling families.

Feeling **Footloose**? This musical is a favorite with kids and teens and now the 80s movie comes to the stage. This is teen rebellion with a toe-tapping storyline. You can call Ticketmaster, *Tel. 702/474-4000, www.ticketmaster.com,* for advance tickets or get them at the Rio Box Office, *Tel. 888/746-7784.* The cost is $45.

If you've got any Elvis buffs in the family, a good choice is **"The Dream King"**, *Holiday Inn Boardwalk, 3750 Las Vegas Boulevard South, Tel. 702/735-1167 or 800/465-4329, Fax 702/739-8152, www.hiboardwalk.com.* The show is a tribute to Elvis and follows him from his early years to his days in the army to his career in Las Vegas. Kids under 12 are free for the show, which is scheduled Tuesday - Saturday at 8:30 p.m. Tickets are $24.95.

If you're visiting during the summer months, another option is the **Children's Summer Concert Series**. For over a decade and a half, this series has entertained children ages five and up with both musical and theatrical performances. Events are held at the **Charleston Heights Arts Center Theater**, *800 S. Brush Street, Tel. 702/229-6383*; call for performance hours.

Certainly one of Las Vegas's largest shows is **EFX**, *MGM Grand Hotel and Casino, 3799 Las Vegas Boulevard South,, 800/929-1111 or 702/891-7777, www.mgmgrand.com*. Pronounced "effects," this show has been named the best in the city several times and continues to pack crowds into the 1700-seat theater. The show once starred David Cassidy but is now showcasing Tony Award winner Tommy Tune. This $45 million show takes its star through time and into contact with everything from dragons to flying saucers. Be prepared to be amazed at this fun show. The show plays twice nightly at 7:30 and 10:30pm, Tuesday through Saturday.

EFX TRIVIA

- *EFX cost $35 million to produce plus an additional $30 million to redesign the theater specially for the show.*
- *The show uses 15,000 cubic feet of liquid nitrogen.*
- *During times of high humidity, the fog moves into the audience.*
- *About 10 pounds of class C explosives are used in each show.*
- *The show's dragons each cost over $1 million.*
- *Morgana, the smaller dragon, was created by the company who created the dinosaurs of Jurassic Park.*

LIGHTS, ACTION, CAMERAS!

Downtown travelers can enjoy the $70 million **Fremont Street Experience**. This unique 175,700-square-foot light and sound show is a pedestrian experience located right on Fremont Street. A 90-foot tall canopy covers four acres of the street. Over two million lights dance across the canopy in a six-minute every hour after dark.

FAMILY APPROPRIATE DINNER SHOWS

One of the most fun family dinner shows in town is the **Tournament of Kings**, *Excalibur, 3850 Las Vegas Boulevard South, Tel. 702/597-7777 or 800/937-7777*. This show combines the excitement of a jousting match with the ease of a dinner show. In the arena, a King Arthur-style show features jousters, wizards, dragons, and plenty of medieval atmosphere. Kids will like the food service, too – it's all enjoyed without cutlery for an authentic medieval dining experience. Tickets are $36.95. Dinner shows are presented twice daily at 6pm and 8:30pm. For reservations or information, call *702/597-7600*.

There's one dinner show in town that's part show and all fun. The **Hawaiian Hot Luau at Imperial Palace** is set up poolside and operates only from April through October, Tuesday and Thursday evenings. The evening starts at 6:30pm with an evening of Polynesian seafood (served at a buffet), unlimited Mai Tai and Pina Coladas as well as non-alcoholic fruit punch, and music and dance with an island flair. The area is lit with torches but the real "lighting" comes with a fire knife dance. Kids can even take part in hula lessons and a sing-a-long. Characters from the hotel's "Legends in Concert" show (above) also drop by. Reservations are required for the luau. Stop by the Show Reservation booth on the first floor or the Shangri-La pool bar or call *702/794-3261*.

RADIO & TELEVISION SHOW

Imperial Palace has another special evening event every Saturday night. From 6-8pm in the Auto Collection, **"Backstage Live"** is aired. The show has all types of different guests and it is broadcast live on Talk America Radio Network and Cable Radio Network, Saturday nights from 6 to 8 p.m. Pacific time and televised on the America Independent Television Network. Admission is free and guests also receive a tour of the Auto Collection. For more, see *www.backstagelive.com.*

MOVIE THEATERS

Movies are more than just films in Las Vegas. Along with traditional movie theaters, you'll find a state of the art theater, **IMAX**, in town, some with specially designed moving seats to let the audience feel like part of the action.

Two 3-D theaters are found at **Sahara Speedworld**, *Sahara, 2535 Las Vegas Boulevard South, Tel. 702/737-2111.* The cost is $3; the facility is open 10am-midnight daily. 3-D theaters are also found at **Cinema Ride**, *The Forum Shops at Caesars Palace, 3500 Las Vegas Boulevard South, Tel. 702/369-4008,* with shows that give you the sensation of flying along in a roller coaster, a spaceship, a submarine, or other exciting vessels but all from the safety of your specially designed theater seat. Tickets are $9.50 for adults, $6.75 for kids 12 and under.

Restrictions: Riders must be at least 42 inches tall.

At **Theaters of Sensation**, *Venetian Resort Hotel Casino, Grand Canal Shoppes, 3377 Las Vegas Boulevard South, Tel. 702/733-0545,* the 3-D motion rides feature five different films that rotate between two screens. The films include a gondola ride, a trip through time to King Tut's Tomb , and others. Combination tickets are available for four films or two films, each which lasts just 10 minutes. The rides are open from 10am-11pm (and to midnight on Friday and Saturday nights).

Restrictions: riders must be 48 inches tall (except for the underwater ride with no motion). The cost is $9 for adults for one ride ($7 for kids).

Yes, you'll find traditional movie theaters here also. **Showcase 8**, *3769 South Las Vegas Boulevard, Tel. 702/225-4828,* offers first-run movies.

At **Orleans**, *4500 W. Tropicana, Tel. 702/365-7111, www.orleanscasino.com,* you'll find a 12-screen movie complex and at the sister hotel, **Gold Coast**, *4000 West Flamingo Road, Tel. 702/ 367-7111 or 800/331-5334, www.goldcoastcasino.com,* you'll find two theaters.

The first IMAX 3-D theater in town was **Luxor IMAX Theatre**, *3900 Las Vegas Boulevard South, Tel. 702/262-4000 or 800/288-1000.* Call for current shows and times. Cost is $8.95.

11. DO WE HAVE TO GO HOME ALREADY?

DAY TRIPS AROUND LAS VEGAS

LAKE MEAD

One of the most popular excursions from Las Vegas is a visit to sprawling Lake Mead and surrounding **Lake Mead National Recreation Area**. Located 25 miles east of the city, this area offers families ample opportunities for boating, camping, swimming, fishing, picnicking, hiking, and exploring the rugged landscape by automobile. The full extent of the Lake Mead NRA is staggering: over one and one-half million acres and includes sections of three of North America's deserts, the Sonoran, Mojave, and Great Basin.

Lake Mead NRA was founded in 1964, but its roots go back to 1931 when a huge dam across Black Canyon was envisioned as a way to assure water supplies, control flooding on the Colorado River, and produce electrical power. The dam's construction was the largest such project to be attempted and was not without controversy. Some critics predicted that the weight of the lake's water would have a disastrous effect on the earth's rotation! However, the can-do attitude of the builders prevailed and the dam was finished in 1935, two years ahead of schedule. Today, families can learn about the dam's fascinating history at the Hoover Dam

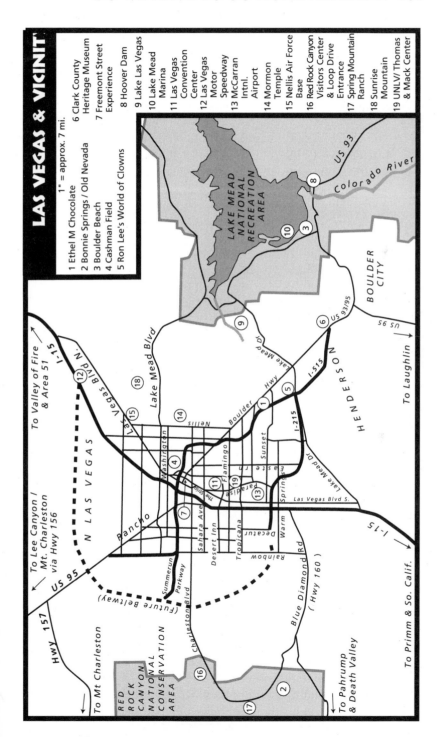

LAS VEGAS & VICINITY

1" = approx. 7 mi.

1 Ethel M Chocolate
2 Bonnie Springs / Old Nevada
3 Boulder Beach
4 Cashman Field
5 Ron Lee's World of Clowns
6 Clark County Heritage Museum
7 Freemont Street Experience
8 Hoover Dam
9 Lake Las Vegas
10 Lake Mead Marina
11 Las Vegas Convention Center
12 Las Vegas Motor Speedway
13 McCarran Intnl. Airport
14 Mormon Temple
15 Nellis Air Force Base
16 Red Rock Canyon Visitors Center & Loop Drive Entrance
17 Spring Mountain Ranch
18 Sunrise Mountain
19 UNLV/ Thomas & Mack Center

Visitor Center, open every day from 8am to 5:45pm. Tours of the dam leave the Center beginning at 8:45am; regular tours take about one-half hour, special hard-hat tours take about an hour.

Even by today's standards, Hoover Dam is impressive: 600 feet thick at its base and rising 730 feet, its turbines producing 4 billion kilowatt hours of electricity each year. Lake Mead is also huge, spanning 158,000 acres with over 550 miles of shoreline. In places, its waters are 500 feet deep and cover plains, canyons, and even a few ghost towns.

Several varieties of bass, rainbow trout, catfish, and assorted panfish thrive in the lake, so fishing is one of the top attractions. Although parents will need to have Nevada and/or Arizona fishing licenses, no license is required on Lake Mead for children under the age of 14. Numerous marinas around the lake can furnish all you will need for a fun day of fishing as well as for other types of watersports: boat rentals, including houseboats, sailboats, sailboards, canoes, and kayaks.

If family members would rather keep their feet dry, there are several recommended driving tours in the area. From the Alan Bible Visitors Center near Boulder City, take Northshore Scenic Drive or Lakeshore Scenic Drive. Both tours offer excellent views of the desert landscape around Lake Mead, including several spectacular rock formations from well-maintained paved roads. Hiking trails allow curious visitors to get an even closer look at the desert. One such trail leads through a canyon with preserved Native American petroglyphs. Hikes can be done with or without park naturalists though all hikers are advised to follow Park Service guidelines, available at the Visitor's Center.

If you want to stretch your day trip into a longer visit, there are several options available for families. There are eight campgrounds and six RV parks with hookups within the Lake Mead NRA as well as several motels near the Area's entrances. For information on camping and other lodging in the area call the Lake Mead NRA, *Tel. 702/293-8990.*

VALLEY OF FIRE

Less than an hour's drive north of the city, Nevada's **Valley of Fire State Park**, *Tel. 702/397-2088,* offers scenic drives and hiking trails. Established in 1935, Valley of Fire was Nevada's first state park and covers some 46,000 acres. Although named for its fantastically colored sandstone formations, the valley becomes firey hot in the summer so hike with caution and plenty of water. Actually, many of its interesting sights can be seen from the comfort of the family automobile and most visitors choose this method.

However, one exception is the short, sandy walk to see Mouse's Tank, named for a Paiute warrior who used the area for a hideout in the late 1800's. Located at the end of Petroglyph Canyon, covered with the drawings by Native American artists, the tank is actually a natural catchbasin for rainwater.

To drive to the park from Las Vegas, take Interstate 15 north for about 35 miles, then take the exit for State Highway 169. Drive east on 169 for about 15 miles and you will see the entrance to the park.

RED ROCK

Red Rock Canyon, *Tel. 702/363-1921,* provides families a nice counterpoint to the neon bustle of Las Vegas. Only a few miles west of the city, the canyon is named for its brilliant sandstone formations, a naturally-occurring display of gaudy colors and shapes. Part of the Spring Mountain range, the canyon's colors range from red to white, with contrasting bands of gray and brown. Red Rock Canyon National Conservation Area features miles of scenic drives and a wide assortment of hiking trails.

The dramatic juxtaposition of different colors in the canyon is the result of a geologic phenomenon called a thrust fault. Millions of years ago two tectonic plates were jammed together with the softer rock in effect wrapping around the older, harder stone.

A good place to begin is at the Red Rock Canyon Visitor's Center. Kids will especially enjoy the hands-on displays which demonstrate the ecology and geology of the area and also the outdoor Desert Tortoise Habitat which features several of the endangered species. Personnel at the Visitor's Center, administered by the Bureau of Land Management, will be able to advise you on the best places to drive, hike, picnic, and take photos.

Some of the best hikes center around the area known as the Calico Hills, named for their wild color scheme. Several trails lead to excellent points from which to view or photograph the surrounding landscapes. Watch for the wild burros!

MT. CHARLESTON

What can you do when the family is tired of Las Vegas' desert heat? Go to the mountains, that's what!

The **Mount Charleston Wilderness** is less than 50 miles away from the Strip, but what a difference an hour's drive makes. You'll discover much cooler temperatures away from the valley floor, sometimes as much as 30 degrees. The highest point, Charleston Peak, stands 11,900 feel tall.

As you drive from the desert, you will enter the Mount Charleston Wilderness, part of the Toiyabe National Forest, thousands of acres of pine and aspen, with lots of chances for sightseeing, picnicking, hiking, horseback riding, and camping. Prime areas to stop and have a cool picnic lunch include the Deer Creek, Old Mill, Cathedral Rock, and Foxtail areas. All of these provide tables, cooking grills, and restroom facilities. Fees are charged at some of the sites and large groups will need to make reservations.

If your family likes to camp, the Mount Charleston area can accommodate you with campgrounds ranging in services from basic to those with more comforts. Several are handicap accessible, as well. However, all campgrounds require reservations by calling 800/280-CAMP.

MOUNT CHARLESTON TEMPERATURE CHART

(High/Low)

Month	High/Low
January	38/10
February	53/13
March	40/17
April	47/21
May	52/28
June	71/41
July	75/42
August	73/42
September	66/35
October	50/22
November	38/10
December	33/10

There are numerous good hiking trails throughout the Wilderness area. The refreshing mountain air, scented with the aroma of the pines, surrounds you and the oppressive heat of the desert floor is just a memory. Established trails range in length from .1 mile to over 10 miles so you can pick the walk best suited to your children's ages and stamina (and yours!) and the amount of time you have available to explore. One short trail, Desert View, is paved for use by wheelchair-bound visitors. On the trails at higher elevations you will see stands of Bristlecone Pines, among the oldest living organisms on earth. Many trails offer glimpses of streams and flowing springs and even waterfalls.

To reach Mount Charleston from Las Vegas, take Highway 95 north to Kyle Canyon, then turn on Highway 157.

ASH MEADOWS NATIONAL WILDLIFE REFUGE

Think the only wildlife in Las Vegas is standing around the nickel slot machines? Think again. About two hours from downtown Las Vegas, you'll find this preserve filled with unique species of plants and animals. To reach the refuge, take I-15 north from the city to US95 North. Continue to Nevada 160 South. Three miles from the town of Pahrump, turn left on Bell Vista Road and continue to the south entrance of the refuge.

What makes this refuge unique is its species, such as the endangered pupfish. This tiny fish is found at a place in the park called Crystal Spring, one protected by the US Fish and Wildlife Service.

Although some areas are protected to ensure the survival of these species, other areas are available for visitor use, including nature trails and picnic areas.

There's no admission fee for visiting the park. The visitors center is open 7am-4:30pm weekdays. For more information, call the Ash Meadows National Wildlife Refuge, *Tel. 775-372-5435.*

CHLORIDE

Want to visit a real mining town? Then set your sights on **Chloride**, located about a 1-1/2 hour drive from downtown. This community, located on the Nevada-Arizona border, is the oldest silver mining camp in Arizona. Once a boomtown, today it is home to only a few hundred residents who live in the foothills.

To reach Chloride, head east on Tropicana to I-515/US 93. Turn east on US 93 and continue to the Arizona border.

Those foothills are home to murals created three decades ago by artist Roy Purcell. Older man-made artifacts remain here as well, ones recalling the town's heydays a century earlier in the 1860s. You can see the original jailhouse from those Wild West days; for a more complete picture of the town's early years you can visit a reconstructed Wild West town downtown. And watch out for those gunfighters; they test their skills on the third Saturday of every month. For more, call the Chloride Visitors Center, *Tel. 520/565-4888*, open from 6am-8pm daily.

FLOYD LAMB STATE PARK

Just 20 miles from the city lies this state park, a beautiful place to get out of town for a few hours and enjoy the desert beauty of this region. We thoroughly enjoyed our visit to this park, which is a real contrast to the glitter and glitz just minutes away.

To reach the park, take US 95 north of town past Ann Road then follow the signs to the park. Admission is $5 per car; the park is open from 8am-7pm.

Once in the park, you'll find picnic spots as well as beautiful ponds well stocked with fish. We especially liked the walking paths.

One of the park's highlights is Tule Springs Ranch, where many fossilized mammoth and bison remains have been found. This region was once a watering hole then later became a private ranch used as a retreat for many movie stars waiting out the six-month residency requirement for divorce in Nevada.

For more on the park, call the Floyd Lamb State Park, *Tel. 702/486-5413.*

EXTRATERRESTRIAL HIGHWAY

It's the stuff of the X-Files, the "**Extraterrestrial Highway.**" Yes, that is the official name of this stretch of US375. Running for almost 100 miles, this corridor runs between Hiko and Warm Springs; to reach it from Las Vegas take I-15 north to US 93 North. At Nevada 375, turn west.

The reason for the alien moniker is that this highway passes what is often called "Area 51," the unofficial area where the public believes military aircraft testing has been conducted – or is that an alien spaceship?

How do you know you're on the ET Highway? Just look for the green road signs, of course.

PRIMM'S THRILL RIDES

Can't get enough of rollercoasters and thrill rides in Las Vegas? Then it's time to make a side trip to Primm, located on the California/Nevada border just half an hour from Las Vegas on I-15 (take Highway exit 1). This community's **Buffalo Bill's**, *31900 Las Vegas Blvd. South, Tel. 702/382-1212,* is home to no less than three wild rides:

• **Desperado**: This rollercoaster brings real coaster buffs from miles around, thanks to its height. Formerly the tallest in the world, this monster is still the tallest coaster in North America, dropping riders 225 feet at one point. Rides cost $6 and run from 10am-11:30pm, until midnight on weekends.

Restrictions: riders must be 48 inches tall.

• **Adventure Canyon**: This flume ride marries the fun of a log ride with the thrill of an Old West shoot'em up. Yes, riders float around on the typical log ride experience then they drift through a shooting gallery and have their chance to shoot targets with a "pistol."

Restrictions: riders need to be 48 inches tall.

• **Turbo Drop**: This ride hoists visitors up 180 feet to drop them like a hot potato at 45mph. Yes, people pay good money for this experience. Riders told us it was fun; we'll have to take their word for it. The cost is $5; the ride operates from 10am-11:30pm on weekdays and until midnight on weekends.

Restrictions: riders need to be 48 inches tall.

GRAPEVINE CANYON

It's not the Grand Canyon (more on that later) but it is close to Las Vegas. **Grapevine Canyon** is located near Laughlin, about an hour from Las Vegas, and it is home to Native American rock art and some pretty desert views.

To reach the canyon, take I-15 north from Las Vegas to US 95 South. Just after Searchlight, take a left at the Laughlin cut-off and continue to mile marker 13. Turn left on Christmas Tree Pass onto a gravel road and continue for two miles.

Park rangers take guided walks out to see the petroglyphs, which are well worth a view. Be sure to bring water for this hike, though; there is no drinking water available (and you're going to need it!)

For more information, give the Laughlin Visitors Center a call, *Tel. 800/452-8445*. There is no admission to the park.

GRAND CANYON

No other destination in the National Park System is as instantly recognizable as the Grand Canyon. Definitely one of the "must sees" in the system, this park offers a variety of activities depending on your adventure level.

Grand Canyon National Park is located off Route 180 about 80 miles northwest of Flagstaff or off Route 64 from I-40 from Williams 60 miles north of the park.

Grand Canyon can be done as a day trip from Las Vegas; several operators run flightseeing tours of the canyon from the city (see Chapter 2 for a rundown of those tours). However, we think the best way to see the canyon is to schedule a few days there with your kids.

Start your visit with a stop at the visitors center on the South Rim, located near Grand Canyon Village to learn more about the creation of this spectacular canyon. The Grand Canyon invites long looks out at the canyon from both the North and South Rims. You'll find many scenic overlooks and one of the best activities is

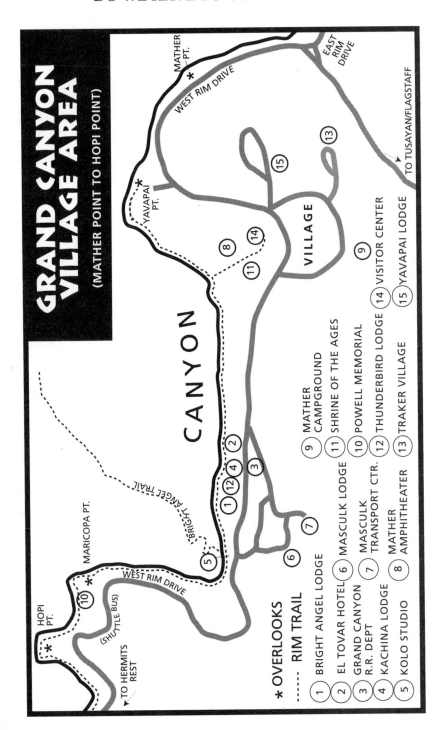

just to look out at the canyon. Watch children carefully at these overlooks, however; drops can be sheer.

Other activities include:

• **Ranger programs**. Interpretive programs for all ages are led daily during peak season. Programs are free; to learn times and subjects check the park newspaper you'll get at the park entrance.

• **Mule Rides**. A fun (although bumpy!) way to explore the canyon is with a full or half day ride by mule. From the North Rim you can take a full or half day trip (from the South Rim you can book a one day or a two-day trip). These don't go all the way to the bottom of the canyon but give you a sense of exploring the region. For reservations, call **Grand Canyon Trail Rides**, *Tel. 435/679-8665.*

• **Overnight Mule Trips**. From the South Rim you can take a two-day, one-night trip down into the Canyon to see the Colorado River. You'll spend the night at Phantom Ranch below the rim. Reservations are a must for these excursions; you can call **AmFac Parks and Resorts**, *Tel. 303/297-2757,* up to 11 months in advance. Only families with older children can take one of these trips, however: all rides must be over 4 feet 7 inches tall (and less than 200 pounds). Also, pregnant vacationers, look elsewhere for activities.

• **Flightseeing**. Air tours are conducted for a true bird's eye view of the canyon. For details, contact **Grand Canyon Chamber of Commerce**, *PO Box 3007, Grand Canyon, AZ 86023.*

• **Bus Tours**. If you'd like to take a guided bus tour to let someone else do the driving for a while, call *303/297-2757* or write **AmFac Parks & Resorts**, *14001 E. Iliff, Aurora, CO 80014.*

If you are like millions of other travelers, you'll be visiting this park from April through October. One of the most popular sites in the park system, Grand Canyon sees five million visitors a year so be prepared for crowds during summer months. Even in off peak months, you'll find crowds on some weekends.

The summer months are beautiful at the canyon, with temperate days that can even be downright chilly thanks to the elevation. Bring layers any time of year. If you visit during the winter, expect snow (and don't be surprised to see snow on the North Rim during fall and spring months as well.)

Before we even start to talk about your lodging options we're going to give you a word of advice: make your reservations early! With five million visitors a year, you can bet that every campsite and lodge room books up. Paris remembers traveling to Grand Canyon with her parents as a child and the family booking a lodge room once they arrived. That was years ago (we won't say how many) and today's travelers don't often have that kind of luck. Make your plans early.

Here are your options for the South Rim. Each of these accommodations are handled by Grand Canyon National Park Lodges. For reservations at any of these properties, call *303/297-2757, Fax 303/297-3175, or write AmFac Parks and Resorts, 14001 E. Iliff, Aurora, CO 80014.*

• **El Tovar.** This is one of the most famous lodges in the national park system, perched right on the South Rim. The lodge was built in 1905 by the Santa Fe Railroad and is worth a visit even if you aren't staying here.

• **Bright Angel Lodge.** Built in 1935, this lodge has hotel rooms as well as cabins, all built in a rustic style. Don't miss the fireplace in the lodge, constructed of rocks that represent each of the geologic periods at the park.

• **Kachina and Thunderbird Lodges**. These lodges are modern and located on the South Rim near El Tovar. Both lodges are identical.

• **Maswik Lodge**. This lodge offers modern rooms similar to a motel. You can choose from motel rooms or cabins (which are closed during the winter season). This lodge is a good choice for those with an eye on the budget.

• **Yavapai Lodge**. This lodge is the largest in the park and offers motel-like accommodations. It's not on the rim but you can walk to the South Rim from your room. It's also near the visitors center as well as the general store and other facilities in Grand Canyon Village.

• **Phantom Ranch**. This lodge is below the canyon rim and offers cabins and dormitory accommodations.

The North Rim also offers accommodations during the season including:

• **Grand Canyon Lodge**. This lodge is right on the rim at Bright Angel Point and offers motel-like accommodations and cabins. The lodge was built in the 1920s features huge windows that overlook the canyon.

For more on the park, contact the **Grand Canyon National Park**, *PO Box 129, Grand Canyon, AZ 86023, Tel. 520/638-7888.*

BRYCE CANYON NATIONAL PARK, UTAH

This southern Utah park has some beautiful formations caused by erosion. A great place for hiking and outdoor photography, this park is also a favorite with those looking for a place to view the night sky far from city lights. It's a bit far for a day trip, but if you're on the way to Salt Lake City from Las Vegas, it's well worth a stop.

The park is located off US89. From US 89, take Utah 12 east to the junction of Utah 12 and 63. Turn south on Utah 63 and continue to the park. If you are traveling from the east, take Utah 12 west to the intersection of Utah 63. Turn south.

The park may seem like it's located a long way from civilization, but if you visit on a peak weekend you'll see that civilization has come to Bryce Canyon. To cut back on the number of cars in the park, the park is instituting a shuttle bus service between mid-May and the end of September. Use of the shuttle isn't mandatory, but if you bring your vehicle in the park you'll have to pay a $5 fee.

Hiking is the top activity in the park, with over 50 miles of trails from which to choose. Families might consider the 1/2 mile walk on Rim Trail between Sunset and Sunrise Points.

Kids ages 12 and under can take part in the Junior Ranger Program here. Children attend a ranger-led activity so they'll need about a day's visit to the park to complete their booklets and pick up a Junior Ranger certificate (or spring for a patch for $1).

The Bryce Canyon Lodge offers guest rooms and cabins from April 1 through the end of October. For reservations, write **Amfac Parks and Resorts, Inc.,** *14001 East Iliff Ave., Suite 600, Aurora, CO 80014 or call 303/297-2757.* Lodging is also available outside the park; for reservations call *800/GO-BRYCE.*

Campers have two options in the park, both on a first-come, first served basis. The campgrounds have no hookups but they're still plenty popular – if you don't get there shortly after lunch you won't get a space.

For more information, contact the **Bryce Canyon National Park**, *PO Box 170001, Bryce Canyon, Utah 84717-0001, Tel. 435/834-5322.*

ARCHES NATIONAL PARK, UTAH

Also in southern Utah, you'll find Arches National Park. Like its name suggests, this park has the largest concentration of sandstone arches in the world. Arches is located in the southern section of Utah near the town of Moab. From Moab, take Utah highway 191 north for five miles.

The main activities here are centered around hiking. Before you head off down the trail, make a stop at the visitors center, located near the park entrance. Here you can watch an orientation program about the park's beautiful formations.

Most families choose to see the park on the road trail. This is a 48-mile trip through the park that takes you to the major attractions for a good view. From the drive, you'll also have the opportunity to pull over and take part in some of the hiking trails.

Some other family activities include hikes with rangers (these are held from March through October so check at the visitors center for times), picnics, and biking – not to mention photographing those spectacular arches. The peak visiting months are March through October. The summer months are toasty at this latitude: expect the mercury to regularly hit 100 degrees during the summer. Bring the sunscreen!

If you visit the park in the winter, plan on opposite extremes. Winter temperatures are often below freezing and can fluctuate over 50 degrees throughout the day.

The park campground, Devils Garden Campground, has 50 tent and trailer sites and these are at a premium during summer months and even as early as mid-March and as late as October. This campground is located 18 miles from the park entrance and the facility includes flush toilets and water, at least until freezing weather. To snag one of these sites in the peak months, you'll need to go by the Visitors Center EARLY in the morning (between 7:30 and 8am) or at the entrance station after 8am. These spots fill up very fast.

If you don't get one of those sites, you'll find other accommodations in the area: **Moab Chamber of Commerce**, *Tel. 801/259-7525* and **St. George Chamber of Commerce**, *Tel. 801-628-1658*. For more on the park, contact **Arches National Park**, *PO Box 907, Moab, UT 84532, Tel. 801/259-8161*.

APPENDIX A:
TOLL-FREE HOTEL GUIDE

Alexis Park Hotel
Tel. 800/582-2228

Arizona Charlie's
Tel. 800/342-2695

AVI Casino
Tel. 800/284-2946

Bally's Las Vegas
Tel. 888/742-9248

Barbary Coast
Tel. 888/227-2279

Bellagio
Tel. 888/987-6667

Binion's Horseshoe
Tel. 800/937-6537

Blair House Suites
Tel. 800/553-9111

Boulder Station
Tel. 800/683-7777

Bourbon Street
Tel. 800/634-6956

Buffalo Bill
Tel. 800/386-7867

Caesars Palace
Tel. 800/634-6001

California
Tel. 800/634-6255

Circus Circus
Tel. 800/444-2472

Colorado Belle
Tel. 800/477-4837

Desert Inn
Tel. 800/634-6906

El Cortez
Tel. 800/634-6703

Excalibur
Tel. 800/937-7777

Fiesta
Tel. 800/731-7333

Fitzgeralds Holiday Inn
Tel. 800/274-5825

Flamingo Hilton LV
Tel. 800/732-2111

Four Queens
Tel. 800/634-6045

Fremont
Tel. 800/634-6182

Frontier
Tel. 800/634-6966

Gold Coast
Tel. 800/331-5334

Gold Spike
Tel. 800/634-6703

Golden Gate
Tel. 800/426-1906

Golden Nugget
Tel. 800/634-3403

Hard Rock Hotel Casino
Tel. 800/473-7625

Harrah's Las Vegas
Tel. 800/634-6765

Holiday Inn Boardwalk
Tel. 800/635-4581

Imperial Palace
Tel. 800/634-6441

Jackie Gaughan's Plaza
Tel. 800/634-6575

Klondike Inn
Tel. 702/739-9351

Lady Luck
Tel. 800/523-9582

Las Vegas Club
Tel. 800/634-6532

Las Vegas Hilton
Tel. 800/732-7117

Luxor Hotel
Tel. 800/288-1000

Main Street Station
Tel. 800/465-0711

Mandalay Bay
Tel. 877/632-7000

Mardi Gras
Tel. 800/634-6501

MGM Grand
Tel. 800/929-1111

Monte Carlo
Tel. 800/311-8999

Nevada Hotel
Tel. 800/637-5777

Nevada Palace
Tel. 800/634-6283

New York-New York
Tel. 888/696-9887

Palace Station
Tel. 800/634-3101

Paris
Tel. 888/266-5687

Rio Hotel & Casino
Tel. 800/752-9746

Riviera
Tel. 800/634-6753

Sahara
Tel. 888/696-2121

Sam's Town
Tel. 800/634-6371

San Remo
Tel. 800/522-7366

Santa Fe
Tel. 800/872-6823

Showboat
Tel. 800/634-3484

Silverton
Tel. 800/588-7711

Stardust
Tel. 800/634-6757

Stratosphere Hotel Casino
Tel. 800/998-6937

Sunset Station
Tel. 888/786-7389

Texas Station
Tel. 800/654-8804

The Mirage
Tel. 800/627-6667

The Orleans
Tel. 800/675-3267

Treasure Island Las Vegas
Tel. 800/944-7444

Tropicana Resort
Tel. 888/826-8767

Venetian
Tel. 888/283-6423

Westward Ho
Tel. 800/634-6803

Whiskey Pete's
Tel. 800/386-7867

APPENDIX B:
LAS VEGAS WEBSITES

GENERAL WEBSITES

www.lasvegas24hours.com
Las Vegas 24 Hours

This is the official website of the Las Vegas Convention and Visitors Authority. You'll find everything from hotels to activities to special events here.

www.lasvegas.com

This extensive site is one of the best, with sections on just about every conceivable Las Vegas-related topic you can imagine, from kids' activities to day trips to sports to relocation. Don't miss this one.

www.todayinlv.com/
Today in Las Vegas Magazine

Check out this website and you can have a free copy of the magazine mailed to you. It reviews all the shows as well as restaurants, special events, places to go, etc.

www.lvchamber.com
Las Vegas Chamber of Commerce

This site includes both business and consumer sections. The consumer side has a great deal of travel information, from transportation to weddings. You'll also find very helpful relocation information here if you're considering a move to Las Vegas.

www.vegas.com

Vegas.com

This extensive site has info on just about everything Vegas-related, from shows and special events to hotels and attractions.

www.in-vegas.com

In-Vegas.com

This site includes hotels, a city guide, travel tips, and more.

www.blackvegas.com

Black Vegas

This African-American site highlights shopping, dining, leisure activities, business, and entertainment in the city.

lasvegas.citysearch.com

This site includes dining, movies, music, sports, yellow pages, news, visitors guide, shopping guide, reservations center, and more.

www.golasvegas.cc

This site includes attractions, a dining guide, activities, real estate, entertainment, car rentals, hotels, casinos, calendar of events, weather, and shopping.

www.lvol.com

Las Vegas Entertainment Guide

Look for hotels and casinos, hotel ratings, recreation, shopping, transportation, show guide, online bookstore, dining, history, wedding information, and more.

www.pcap.com/lasvegas.htm

A Las Vegas Leisure Travel Visitor's Guide

Check out attractions, tour reservations, businesses, hotels, maps, night life, dining, weather, shopping, tickets, recreation, and vehicle rental here.

las.vegas.metroguide.net
Las Vegas Metroguide
This site includes a hotel guide, events, dining, nightlife, shopping, flights and fare guide, new or used car guide, and real estate informatin.

www.las-vegas-guide.com
Las Vegas Information Guide
casinos, insiders tips, hotel guide, quick rate check, dining guide, entertainment guide, attractions, travel information, guided tour information, car rental information, shopping, and more.

www.in-vegas.com
This site includes hotels, casinos, downtown hotels, off-strip hotels and casinos, map of the strip

www.las.vegas.hotelguide.net
This site allows you to search for a hotel by location: the Strip, Airport/University, Henderson, Greater Las Vegas, Convention Center, or by hotel name.

www.bookvegas.com
Book a hotel room, show tickets, car rentals, tours and more.

www.bestreadguide.com/lasvegas
Order airline tickets, hotel rooms, car rentals, show tickets. Find out about Las Vegas attractions, dining, lodging, trandsportation, shopping, events and more.

AIRPORT
mccarran.com/
McCarran International Airport
Get information on flights, the airport, and parking.

CHILD-RELATED WEBSITES

www.child.net/lvkids.htm
Las Vegas City Kids
   This site is a service of the National Children's Coalition and Streetcats Foundation. Here you'll find all kinds of helpful child-related phone services, from hotlines to the public library.

CITY RESOURCES

www.lvccld.lib.nv.us
Las Vegas-Clark Country Library District
   This site is a good resource for new residents, with information on library policies as well as links to community resources.

www.ci.las-vegas.nv.us
City of Las Vegas
   Much of this site is business-oriented, but you will find good information here on public parks, neighborhoods, and getting around town.

www.accessnv.com/henderson
City of Henderson

www.ci.las-vegas.nv.us
City of Las Vegas

www.accessnv.com/bclibrary
Boulder City, NV Library

www.lvmpd.com
Las Vegas Metropolitan Police Department

EDUCATIONAL RESOURCES

www.interact.k12.nv.us
Clark County School District
    A good resource for those thinking of moving with kids to Las Vegas.

www.unlv.edu
UNLV
    The website of the University of Nevada, Las Vegas includes links to museums and galleries, the performing arts center, and more.

www.ccsn.nevada.edu
Community College of Southern Nevada

HOTELS & MOTELS

www.nvhotels.com
Nevada Hotel and Motel Association
    This on-line lodging guide covers over 60,000 hotel rooms in Nevada.

www.ballyslv.com
Bally's

www.coastcasinos.com/barbary/
Barbary Coast

www.bellagiolasvegas.com
Bellagio - The Resort

www.boulderstation.com
Boulder Station

www.caesars.com
Caesars Palace

www.thecal.com
California

www.circuscircus.com
Circus Circus

www.econolodgelasvegas.com
Econo Lodge - Downtown

www.elcortez.net
El Cortez Hotel & Casino

www.excalibur-casino.com
Excalibur

vegas.fitzgeralds.com
Fitzgerald's

www.lv-flamingo.com
Flamingo Hilton

www.fourqueens.com
Four Queens

www.fourseasons.com/lasvegas
Four Seasons Hotel Las Vegas

www.coastcasinos.com/goldcoast
Gold Coast

www.goldennugget.com
Golden Nugget

www.hardrockhotel.com
Hard Rock Hotel and Casino

harrahs.lv.com
Harrah's Casino Hotel

www.hawthorn.com
Hawthorn Suites

www.hiboardwalk.com
Holiday Inn Boardwalk

www.sanremolasvegas.com
Hotel San Remo Casino and Resort

www.lakelasvegas.hyatt.com
Hyatt Regency- Lake Las Vegas

www.imperialpalace.com
Imperial Palace

www.laquinta.com
La Quinta

www.laquinta.com
La Quinta (Strip)

www.ladyluck.com/lasvegas/index.html
Lady Luck

www.playatlvc.com
Las Vegas Club Hotel and Casino

www.lvhilton.com
Las Vegas Hilton

www.luxor.com/
Luxor

www.mainstreetcasino.com
Main Street Station

www.mandalaybay.com
Mandalay Bay

www.mgmgrand.com
MGM Grand

www.mirage.com
Mirage

www.monte-carlo.com/main.htm
Monte Carlo

www.mtcharlestonhotel.com
Mount Charleston Inn

www.nevadalanding.com
Nevada Landing

www.pcap.com/nvpalace.htm
Nevada Palace Hotel and Casino

www.frontierlv.com
New Frontier

www.nynyhotelcasino.com
New York - New York

www.orleanscasino.com
Orleans

www.palacestation.com
Palace Station

www.paris-lv.com/
Paris

www.keylargocasino.com
Quality Inn - Key Largo

www.playrio.com
Rio

www.theriviera.com
Riviera

www.pcap.com/sahara.htm
Sahara

www.fremontcasino.com
Sam Boyd's Fremont Hotel and Casino

www.samstownlv.com
Sam's Town

www.santafecasino.com
Santa Fe

www.stardustlv.com
Stardust

www.sttropezlasvegas.com
St. Tropez

www.sunsetstation.com
Sunset Station

www.texasstation.com
Texas Station

www.treasureislandlasvegas.com
Treasure Island

tropicanalv.com
Tropicana

vacationvillagevegas.com
Vacation Village

venetian.com
The Venetian

www.westwardho.com
Westward Ho Hotel and Casino

NEVADA TOURISM INFORMATION
www.travelnevada.com
State Of Nevada Tourism

www.state.nv.us
State Of Nevada

PUBLICATIONS

www.lvshowbiz.com
Showbiz: The Ultimate Guide to Las Vegas Entertainment
This site includes both shows and dining; special features spotlight some of the city's top entertainers.

www.lasvegassun.com
Las Vegas Sun
This site includes the day's top stories as well as features on topics of special interest to families like Vegas rollercoasters.

www.lasvegasweekly.com
Las Vegas Weekly
This site includes a city guide and a comprehensive calendar of events.

www.lvlife.com
Las Vegas Life
This magazine includes special features on Las Vegas life, for both residents and visitors.

www.lvrj.com/
Las Vegas Review-Journal
This newspaper site includes top stories as well as features and community information.

RADIO STATIONS

www.knpr.org
KNPR 89.5

www.kcepfm88.com
KCEP 88.1

www.intermind.net/kedg
KEDG 103.5

www.komp.com/komp
KOMP 92.3

www.vegasradio.com/kool.html
KOOL 105.5

www.xtremeradio.com/
KXTE 107.5

SPECIAL EVENTS

www.thomasandmack.com
Thomas and Mack Center

www.lasvegastickets.com
Las Vegas Tickets Service
This company sells tickets to all the Las Vegas shows, if you're interested in booking a particular show before your trip.

www.ticketmaster.com
Ticketmaster
Many of the larger shows and special events offer their tickets through Ticketmaster; you can purchase tickets online.

TELEVISION STATIONS

www.kvbc.com
KVBC, Channel 3 (NBC)

www.klas-tv.com
KLAS, Channel 8 (CBS)

www.ktnv.com
KNTV, Channel 13 (ABC)

www.kfbt.com
KFBT Channel 33

www.wb21.com
WB Channel 21

JEAN & PRIMM HOTELS

(see Chapter 11)

www.primadonna.com
Buffalo Bill's

www.goldstrike-jean.com
Gold Strike Hotel and Gambling Hall

www.nevadalanding.com
Nevada Landing

www.primadonna.com
Primm Valley Resort

www.primadonna.com
Whiskey Pete's

E-MAIL NEWSLETTERS

Viva Las Vegas Newsletter is an excellent source of information on who's playing in the city, new openings, and more. The free newsletter is available by e-mail. To get on the mailing list, send an e-mail to *billhere@lvcm.com*. On the subject line of your note, type "subscribe."

APPENDIX C: LAS VEGAS DIRECTORY

AUTOMOBILE REPAIR

1st Gear Transmission Service
3820 E. Craig Rd.
Tel. 702/ 644-1515

ALS Discount Auto and Tire
1623 North Main Street
Tel. 702/ 642-4868

Preferred Automotive Services
3824 Losee Rd.
Tel. 702/ 649-4499

Royal Auto Center
2610 Las Vegas Blvd. North
Tel. 702/ 399-5233

HOSPITALS & MEDICAL CENTERS

Center For Healthy Families
3100 N. Tenaya Way
Tel. 702/233-5326

Desert Springs Hospital
2075 E. Flamingo Road
Tel. 702/733-8800

Fremont Medical Center
331 N. Buffalo Dr.
Tel. 702/228-5477

Montevista Hospital
5900 W. Rochelle Ave.
Tel. 702/364-1111

Mountain View Hospital
3100 N. Tenaya Way
Tel. 702/255-5000

Saint Rose Urgent Care
1776 E. Warm Springs Road
Tel. 702/914-7100

Summerlin Hospital Medical Center
657 N. Town Center Dr.
Tel. 702/233-7000

Sunrise Children's Hospital
3186 S. Maryland Pkwy.
Tel. 702/731-8000

Sunrise Hospital & Medical Center
3186 S. Maryland Pkwy.
Tel. 702/731-8000

UMC Quick Care Center
4180 S. Rainbow Boulevard # 810
Tel. 702/248-8877

University Medical Center
1800 W. Charleston Boulevard
Tel. 702/383-2000

Valley Hospital Medical Center
620 Shadow Lane
Tel. 702/388-4000

Vencor Hospital Las Vegas
5110 W. Sahara Ave.
Tel. 702/871-1418

PET BOARDING

Animal Inn Kennels
3460 W. Oquendo Road
Tel. 702/736-0036

A-VIP Kennels
6808 La Cienega St
Tel. 702/361-8900

Cat's Cradle
5650 W. Charleston Boulevard # 1
Tel. 702/457-0370

Creature Comforts Pet Sitting
8101 W. Flamingo Road
Tel. 702/364-4733

Gentle Doctor Animal Hospital
1550 S. Rainbow Boulevard
Tel. 702/259-9200

Hap-E Dog Inn
2225 N. Nellis Boulevard
Tel. 702/452-1963

South Shores Animal Hospital
8420 W. Lake Mead Boulevard
Tel. 702/255-8050

Sue Zan Kennels
1788 N. Gateway Road
Tel. 702/452-7305

Tolgate Kennels
2670 Betty Lane
Tel. 702/643-1015

Veterinary Center Animal Hospital
541 S. Martin L. King Boulevard
Tel. 702/382-4080

INDEX

TRAVEL NOTES

TRAVEL NOTES

TRAVEL NOTES

OPEN ⬤ ROAD PUBLISHING

U.S.A.

America's Cheap Sleeps, $16.95
America's Grand Hotels, $14.95
America's Most Charming Towns &
    Villages, $17.95
Arizona Guide, $16.95
Boston Guide, $13.95
California Wine Country Guide, $12.95
Colorado Guide, $16.95
Disneyworld With Kids, $14.95
Florida Guide, $16.95
Hawaii Guide, $18.95
Las Vegas Guide, $14.95
National Parks With Kids, $14.95
New Mexico Guide, $16.95
San Francisco Guide, $16.95
Southern California Guide, $18.95
Spa Guide U.S.A., $14.95
Texas Guide, $16.95
Utah Guide, $16.95
Vermont Guide, $16.95

MIDDLE EAST/AFRICA

Egypt Guide, $17.95
Israel Guide, $17.95
Jerusalem Guide, $13.95
Kenya Guide, $18.95

UNIQUE TRAVEL

Celebrity Weddings & Honeymoon
    Getaways, $16.95
The World's Most Intimate Cruises, $16.95

SMART HANDBOOKS

The Smart Home Buyer's
    Handbook, $16.95
The Smart Runner's Handbook, $9.95

LATIN AMERICA & CARIBBEAN

Bahamas Guide, $13.95
Belize Guide, $16.95
Bermuda Guide, $14.95
Caribbean Guide, $21.95
Caribbean With Kids, $14.95
Chile Guide, $18.95
Costa Rica Guide, $17.95
Ecuador & Galapagos Islands Guide, $17.95
Guatemala Guide, $18.95
Honduras & Bay Islands Guide, $16.95

EUROPE

Austria Guide, $15.95
Czech & Slovak Republics Guide, $18.95
France Guide, $16.95
Greek Islands Guide, $16.95
Holland Guide, $16.95
Ireland Guide, $17.95
Italy Guide, $19.95
London Guide, $14.95
Moscow Guide, $16.95
Paris Guide, $13.95
Portugal Guide, $16.95
Prague Guide, $14.95
Rome & Southern Italy Guide, $14.95
Scotland Guide, $17.95
Spain Guide, $18.95
Turkey Guide, $18.95

ASIA

China Guide, $21.95
Japan Guide, $19.95
Philippines Guide, $18.95
Tahiti & French Polynesia Guide, $18.95
Tokyo Guide, $13.95
Thailand Guide, $18.95
Vietnam Guide, $14.95

To order any Open Road book, send
us a check or money order for the price
of the book(s) plus $3.00 shipping
and handling for domestic orders, to:
Open Road Publishing, PO Box 284,
Cold Spring Harbor, NY 11724